THE
GAMBIA

THE
GAMBIA

THE UNTOLD DICTATOR YAHYA JAMMEH'S STORY

Pa Nderry M'Bai

iUniverse, Inc.
Bloomington

THE GAMBIA
THE UNTOLD DICTATOR YAHYA JAMMEH'S STORY

iUniverse books may be ordered through booksellers or by contacting:

iUniverse
1663 Liberty Drive
Bloomington, IN 47403
www.iuniverse.com
1-800-Authors (1-800-288-4677)

ISBN: 978-1-4759-6154-6 (sc)
ISBN: 978-1-4759-6155-3 (ebk)

Library of Congress Control Number: 2012921352

Printed in the United States of America

iUniverse rev. date: 11/09/2012

CONTENTS

Acknowledgements..vii

References: ix

Chapter One   The Murder of Journalist Deyda Hydara 1

Chapter Two   Rsm Malick Jatta's Reacts to Allegations
                   That He is an Assassin for Jammeh..................17

Chapter Three   Dawda Nyassi Murdered...................................26

Chapter Four   Jammeh Executed First Batch of
                   Death Row Inmates...41

Chapter Five   The Aftermath of the Execution of the
                   Death Row Inmates...57

Chapter Six   Editor M'bai's London Maiden Speech.............80

Chapter Seven   Editor M'bai July 22nd Military Takeover
                   Maiden Speech 86

Chapter Eight   Who Is President Yahya Jammeh? 90

Chapter Nine   A Tribute To Dot Faal And The Fallen
                   November 11 Soldiers 102

Chapter Ten   Signs of Civil War in the Gambia 105

Chpater Eleven   Gambia is a Drug Hub Nation 110

Chapter Twelve   Gambia's Vice President on Journalist
                     Deyda Hydara's Murder 115

Chapter Thirteen   The Most Significant Events in Us's History ...135

Chapter Fourteen   End Impunity in the Gambia 147

Chapter Fifteen   Dr. Amadou Scattered Janneh Speaks 157

About The Author..169

ACKNOWLEDGEMENTS

This book helps to highlight some of the unexplained murder mysteries committed under dictator Yahya Jammeh's administration. It is an account of atrocities allegedly committed by an African despot reputed for his flagrant disregard for human rights, the rule of law, and good governance. The book also provides a vivid account of the situation of governance and press freedom in the Gambia. Mr. M'Bai's book featured the compilation of his published journalistic work on his online www.Freedomnewspaper.com publication. It's a non-fictional book.

My sincere thanks and appreciation goes out to all sources, who volunteered information during my research. Mr. M'Bai's book contains vital information, which could be useful to human rights researchers, students, and academicians interested in Gambian related matters.

REFERENCES:

Freedom Newspaper: www.freedomnewspaper.com

Gambia Government Press Release

Rev. Jesse Jackson, Sr's Letter to Jammeh

www.foxnews.com

Caruso Kevin. The Vietnam War. Retrieved From: http://www.vietnammemorial.com/vietnam-war.html

Learn about the Vietnam War. Retrieved June 20 2009 From:http://www.digitalhistory.uh.edu/modules.cfm

http://www.colorado.edu/AmStudies/lewis/2010/mccarthy.htm

Stephen Budiansky Stephen, Goode E. Erica, Gest Ted. (January 24 1994) The Cold War experiments. Retrieved May 23 2009 From: http://www.geocities.com/area51/shadowlands/6583/project120.html

Saul Michale. (July 16, 2009) President Obama honors civil rights pioneers with speech at NAACP centennial convention http://www.nydailynews.com/news/politics/2009/07/16/2009-07-16_president_obama_honors_civil_rights_pioneers_with_speech_at_naacp_centennial_con.html

Moody Kim. Reagan, The business Agenda and the collapse of labor. Retrieved July 16 2009 From: http://66.102.1.104/scholar?q=cache: rSF4wJWzfj4J:scholar.google.com/+corporate+greed+during+Reagan &hl=en

CHAPTER ONE

THE MURDER OF JOURNALIST DEYDA HYDARA

Gambia's iron fist dictator President Yahya Jammeh has been allegedly named in the murder of Mr. Deyda Hydara, the Founding Editor, and Co Proprietor of the Point Newspaper. Mr. Hydara was murdered in December of 2004 by security agents allegedly acting under the instructions of President Yahya Jammeh. The Kanilai born dictator has repeatedly denied his alleged involvement in the murder of Mr. Hydara. Mr. Hydara's murder devastated the entire world. It provoked both local and international outcry—with the international community denouncing the highhandedness of dictator Jammeh's regime. The main motive behind the murder of Hydara, according to administration sources, was largely due to his critical newspaper commentaries and news analysis against the Jammeh administration. Mr. Hydara's writings were widely deemed in some quarters within the administration as "completely distasteful and totally out of place," in a country, in which the Gambian dictator claims to be in total control.

Dissent, in whatever form, it is considered as a crime under Jammeh's rule. And the late Deyda Hydara has paid very dearly for merely exercising his dissenting views against a dictatorship, which is notorious for its total disregard for human rights, the rule of law, and the freedom of the press.

Three Gambian journalists have so far been killed since the advent of Jammeh's rule: Deyda Hydara, Pa Omar Barrow, a former Red Cross Volunteer, also a former Editor of the Banjul based Sud FM Radio, and Ebrima Chief Manneh. Press Houses critical of his government

1

are often shutdown, fire bombarded, and in some occasions detained journalists are exposed to brutal torture.

It took Mr. Hydara's killers months to strategize, and coordinate for his murder. Interior Minister Ousman Sonko, alongside with the late Captain Tumbul Tamba, the former head of Jammeh's alleged secret assassin team in Banjul were summoned to a meeting to discuss the murder plot that was hatched against the Gambian journalist. Mr. Sonko was bit reluctant to execute the mission—given the local, and international outcry Hydara's murder could have attracted if the assassin team should have carried out the President's alleged assignment as instructed. But dictator Jammeh, we have been told, allegedly insisted that the murder of Hydara must be executed by any means necessary. He even went to the point of threatening Ousman Sonko with possible arrest and imprisonment if the murder mission of Hydara was not accomplished, our sources alleged.

Mr. Sonko, a former police chief, and also a retired army officer, mobilizes the assassin team under his direct command to brief them about what needed to be done to execute Mr. Jammeh's alleged orders. He relayed Jammeh's message exactly: word for word to the assassin team as he was allegedly instructed by his boss Yahya Jammeh, the commander-in-chief of Gambia's Armed Forces. Mr. Jammeh wants Mr. Deyda Hydara dead, our sources further alleged. No questions were asked as to what might have necessitated the President's alleged order. The men headed by Sonko went ahead to execute the mission to take Hydara's life under the cover of darkness.

Deyda's murder plot was considered in some quarters within the administration, as one of the toughest assignments ever given to Ousman Sonko allegedly by dictator Jammeh. Mr. Sonko couldn't afford to fail his boss. Failure means the end of Sonko's career! That was one the reasons why Sonko was determined to exceed Jammeh's expectations.

Mr. Sonko, who was a former Army Signal officer, before being enlisted into Jammeh's secret murder syndicate, is an alleged career hit man. He has been accused of allegedly coordinating Jammeh's secret murder machine in the Gambia. He often drives around town with vehicles without registration number.

A former army officer, who worked with Mr. Sonko at the State House in Banjul, has alleged that Mr. Sonko's involvement into the secret assassination of Gambians is a public knowledge. "I happen to swing by Sonko's office one fine morning and found seven mask helmets hidden in his closet. The masks I saw on the day in question are usually used by armed robbers, or serial killers. There were also videotapes of soldiers training found in Sonko's office. He has been executing secret killings for the President. Sonko and his team killed the late Lieutenant Almamo Manneh," the Army officer alleged. "President Jammeh is a reactionary leader. He has been using the likes of Sonko to kill our people for nothing. He has been very involved in the arrest, torture, and disappearances of perceived political opponents in the country. Almost all the arrest, tortures, and secret executions carried out in this country are sanctioned by Jammeh. He personally instructed me to kill Ousainanou Darboe, a prominent Gambian politician, but I advised him to resolve the matter amicably," the former army officer alleged.

The President wanted Mr. Darboe dead because one of his party supporters was killed in Basse. There was a political tension in the Basse area between the supporters of the Ruling APRC and the main opposition United Democratic Party (UDP). The political violence led to the killing of an APRC driver, one Alieu Njie, who was beaten to death.

The former Army officer said President Jammeh wanted to avenge the murder of Alieu Njie. He was allegedly instructed by the President to ambush Ousainanou Darboe's convoy on their way to Banjul and possibly kill the opposition leader. At the time, he said, the late Baba Kajali Jobe, the former Chairman of the July 22nd Movement had also mobilized his followers to attack the UDP convoy. The army chief said he saved Mr. Darboe's life because if he had executed the President's orders as instructed, Mr. Darboe would have been dead by now. The officer had a contingent of soldiers under his command at the time.

The President ordered me to kill Mr. Darboe, and his entourage, but I was able to convince him to reconsider his decision, the army officer alleged. The army officer met Mr. Darboe and his supporters in Basse during the political tension. He assured Mr. Darboe that he was there to protect them. The tension was charged at the material time. The APRC supporters and their leader Baba Jobe were determined to avenge Alieu Njie's murder. Mr. Darboe told the officer that his safety and that of his supporters was in his hands. The UDP delegation was escorted to Banjul safely without any problem.

The UDP leader Ousainou Darboe and dozen of his followers were charged for the murder of Mr. Njie. Journalist Mady Ceesay, the Proprietor of the Daily News Newspaper was among those charged by 7the state. The case was later dropped, following the intervention of some Western Diplomats accredited to Banjul.

President Jammeh told his supporters shortly after the execution of the nine death row inmates that the opposition leader was very lucky to be pardoned, otherwise he would have been among the first batch of inmates, who were killed through lethal injection. He said he received numerous appeals from local diplomats to drop Darboe's murder case. He told his supporters that Mr. Darboe would have been dead by now if he was found guilty and sentenced to death by the court.

Earning his fame, following his delusional fake claim of having the cure for aids, asthma, diabetes, infertility, and other ailments—amid strong condemnation from anti HIV/AIDS activists around the world, the Gambian despot uses his ill gotten wealth to entice his guards. He ensured that they are well fed, paid, and properly taken care of.

Mr. Jammeh is a manipulative leader. The majority of Jammeh's alleged assassin team members are alcoholic, drug addicts, or mentally challenged soldiers. He is exploiting their vulnerabilities to perpetrate crimes against humanity, one of our sources alleged. They execute all kinds of missions assigned to them by the dictator. These are young vulnerable soldiers under the manipulation of a despot. Mr. Jammeh made them to believe that it's legal to kill folks perceived as opponents, or enemies of his regime, he further alleged.

On the eve of Hydara's murder, Mr. Sonko was allegedly allocated with enough cash, mobility, and arms by dictator Jammeh to execute the mission. He ensured that Mr. Hydara was placed under constant surveillance days prior to his killing. Deyda was a dead man walking. He was being closely watched from his home, office, and elsewhere across the country.

Mr. Sonko was the main man coordinating the surveillance team. He followed Mr. Hydara as soon as Mr. Hydara left the premises of the Point Newspaper on the night of his murder, while the assassin team was riding in two different Benz taxis. Sonko kept them abreast over the phone about Mr. Hydara's driving directions.

Once Mr. Hydara drove past Jimpex, and was about to reach the Police Intervention Unit Barracks junction, Colonel Kawsu Camara, now a death row inmate, who was riding with Captain Tumbul Tamba and others, hurriedly blocked Hydara's car with his Benz. At this time, WO2 Bai Lowe was trailing Hydara with another Benz Taxi, while riding with Malick Jatta, Sanna Manjang, and co. Sanna Manjang then open fire on Hydara at a close range. Malick Jatta fired the shots that killed Hydara. About six soldiers participated in the murder of Hydara.

Incidentally, Mr. Sonko's second wife was a reporter at the Point Newspaper. She later secured a job with the state controlled television GRTS after the murder of Hydara. She left the paper months after Hydara was murdered. Mr. Sonko's wife was very familiar with the Point's internal editorial operations.

As an Interior Minister, Mr. Sonko is responsible for the country's internal and external security. His primary duty is to ensure that there is peace, stability, and tranquility in the Gambia. Yet, the Interior Minister is the alleged coordinator of dictator Jammeh's secret assassin team. That tells a lot about the type of government running the state of affairs in Banjul. It's a criminal government headed by an irrational leader—known for his erratic tendencies. Mr. Jammeh is said to be mentally unstable.

Mr. Jammeh has been accused of allegedly killing his own brother Haruna Jammeh after accusing him of trying to harm him (Jammeh) spiritually. Marcie Jammeh, a relative of President Jammeh was reported to have made some comments critical of the Head of State shortly after the March 2006 failed coup attempt, and was arrested. She was also killed.

Like Marcie Jammeh, the Kujabi brothers of Bwiam also ran out of luck with Jammeh. Mr. Jammeh allegedly ordered for the arrest of Jasaja Kujabi, after he was fed with information that Jasaja was also trying to hurt him spiritually. Jammeh instructed Ousman Tamaba, the former NIA Western Division Commander to arrest Jasaja. Days later, the President instructed his alleged hit men to pick up Jasaja from NIA custody. Jasaja Kujabi was later murdered. The remains of Jasaja Kujabi, Haruna Jammeh, and Marcie Jammeh were dumped in a well in Kanilai, the President home village, our sources alleged.

There are many unresolved murder mysteries committed under Jammeh's watch. From the late Deyda Hydara, Lieutenant Almamo Manneh, Journalist Ebrima Chief Manneh, Sergeant Ello Gina Jallow, Daba Marena, Ebou Lowe, RSM Alpha Bah, Malafi Corr, Mustapha Colley, Jasaja Kujabi, Haruna Jammeh, Marcie Jammeh, Dawda Nyassi, Ousman Koro Ceesay, Gambia's former Finance Minister, just to name a few.

A charming African despot, Mr. Jammeh prides himself as the supreme leader of the Gambia. He has been accused of allegedly killing an unimaginable number of Gambians, and non Gambians alike since coming to power in July of 1994. He is Africa's most autocratic leader in living memory. Jammeh's alleged crimes against humanity has been widely underreported by Gambia's local media—largely due to his total monopoly of the country's public and private press. There are draconian press laws put in place to muzzle the press. Media houses critical of his regime are often fire bombarded and in some occasions shutdown.

A member of President Jammeh's alleged assassin team, who witnessed Deyda Hydara's murder, confessed to me in a lengthy telephone conversation that Mr. Jammeh allegedly assigned them to kill the late journalist. Audio conversations I had with the confessing soldier have been archived for posterity in the event dictator Jammeh is deposed from power, and is placed on trial for the alleged crimes he committed against the Gambian people. The tapes would be made available to any credible law court, or law enforcement agencies if requested in the interest of the public.

I was introduced to Jammeh's secret assassin soldier by a source—Jammeh himself might not even expect, or suspect that he will have access to such an intelligent asset. This is an interesting world—thanks to the unprecedented evolution of modern communication. I was able to interview a wide range of sources. I mean credible and knowledgeable sources familiar with Jammeh's alleged organized murder syndicate in Banjul.

Given Gambia's precarious security situation, and Jammeh's bad reputation of allegedly killing folks he suspects of compromising his secrets to the media, some of these sources have pleaded with me to protect their identities. Some are still in the military, while others have left the Force.

Narrating how Jammeh allegedly instructed them to take the life of Deyda Hydara, the soldier alleged: "We were instructed by President Yahya Jammeh on the eve of the Point Newspaper anniversary back in December 16th 2004, to shoot and kill the paper's Managing Editor Deyda Hydara. We rode on three taxi vehicles owned by President Jammeh, which was allocated to our team to execute the mission to take the life of Mr. Hydara. I was part of the team that followed Mr. Hydra, and the other passengers on board his vehicle at the material time. I was accompanied by **Major Sana Manjang**, Ex Army Colonel Kawsu Camara, alias (Bombaredeh), **Malick Jatta**, and co while Interior **Minister Ousman Sonko** coordinated the entire operation."

The soldier alleged that Mr. Jammeh designed the murder scheme of Hydara in such a way that it would not look like the Government carried out the incident. In doing so, the President allegedly armed them with local a handgun which is not used by the Gambian military. The bullets that killed Hydara are usually used by local hunters. The Gambian military does not use such bullets, or handguns.

"We were armed with double barrel guns. This type of weapon is not part of the Gambia Armed Forces weaponry. The President personally instructed us to use the double barrel guns to avoid the army being linked to the incident. It was a well coordinated operation," the self confessed soldier alleged.

Dressed in his elegant executive suit that night, while commemorating his paper's thirteen years anniversary, the friendly; and jovial Mr. Deyda Hydara, was in the midst of Western Diplomats—notably the former United States Ambassador to the Gambia, family members, friends, and colleagues in the media fraternity discussing the challenges, successes, and shortcomings recorded by his paper over the years.

It was a night of rejoice for Deyda and his dynamic team at the Point. It was a night of celebrations. Thirteen years of publication is a major success story for the Point—given the lack of press freedom in the Gambia, coupled with the exorbitant cost associated with running a newspaper in Banjul. Newspapers operate under very difficult circumstances in the Gambia. Most Newspapers derived their revenue mainly from advertisement. The majority of the advertisers prefer to advertize with media outlets affiliated with the state.

Days before his murder, Mr. Hydara has spoken publicly about his opposition to a new media law passed by the regime. The new law requires media houses and journalists to register with the Media Commission. The Commission members were mainly Government handpicked appointees. The Commission enjoyed sweeping powers: For example, it is empowered to order for the arrest of journalists, imprisonment, and a worst case scenario—the closure of newspapers.

In Deyda's own views, he thinks that the Media Commission Bill was an unjust law, which should not be obeyed by any independent minded journalist. He made his views very clear to the authorities including President Jammeh. The late journalist made it abundantly clear that he rather seizes to publish his paper than to allow his fate to be decided by a Commission whose independence and impartiality was highly questionable. Mr. Hydara also believes that it is only the courts that should be given the mandate to make legal pronouncements, or pass judgment on the work of journalists and not a Government constituted Commission whose allegiance lies to the Government. He was a strong opponent of the Media Commission Bill. This was evident on his numerous editorials and commentaries calling on the regime to repeal the law. Mr. Hydara has consistently argued that the Media Commission bill is a bad law, which should not be allowed to prevail in any democratic dispensation.

Former administration officials, such as Fatou Jahoumpa Ceesay, the erstwhile State House Director of Press, repeatedly complained about Hydara's "Good Morning Mr. President," column. The column addresses pertinent daily issues affecting the lives of Gambians. Ms. Fatou Jahumpa Ceesay, is the daughter of the late Banjul politician IM Garba Jahumpa. She dislikes Hydara's popular column. She erroneously argued that Mr. Hydara was out to bring President Jammeh's Government down with what she characterizes as Hydara's hateful writings against the President. FJC, as she is fondly called in Banjul, went as far as appealing to the Government to stop Mr. Hydara by any means necessary. She said Hydara has been vilifying the President for no just reasons and should be stopped.

Months after FJC'S denunciation of Hydara's journalistic work, Mr. Hydara was killed. The two other female Point staffers travelling with Hydara at the time of the incident narrowly escaped death when gunmen ambushed Mr. Hydara's vehicle. Mr. Hydara died on the spot, and the remaining passengers were flown out of the country to neighboring Senegal for medical treatment.

The alleged Jammeh assassin team member explained how Hydara was ambushed by his colleagues: "When Deyda Hydara drove passed Jimpex in Kanifing, near the police Intervention barracks, our assault team then launched an attack on his vehicle. **Sana Manjang** first open fire at Mr. Hydara at a close range. Wo2 **Malick Jatta**, the brother of the former Army Chief of Staff Baboucarr Jatta, then fired the shots that killed Mr. Hydara. The Point Boss was killed by Malick Jatta's shots."

"The two other point female staffers, who were riding with Hydara at the time, were not our primary target. Mr. Hydara was our target. We were given instructions by the Head of State Yahya Jammeh to murder Hydra. The order was given to one of our ring leaders, and was filtered down to us for execution," the soldier alleged.

The self confessed alleged Jammeh hit man said he sometimes wonders when he watched Mr. Jammeh on national television lying to the teeth—trying to deny his alleged involvement in the murder of Hydara. He alleged that Mr. Jammeh instructed them to kill Hydara.

After killing Mr. Hydra, the alleged Jammeh assassin team member said they retreated from the scene of the crime, and drove passed the Kanifing garage (Swegam)—next to the President's warehouse. That's where we normally park the three yellow Benz taxis the President bought for our men, he said. The Gambian President owned many warehouses within the Greater Banjul area. He is into rice, cement, oil, sugar, meat, sand, and building materials sale.

"I could vividly remember when he the (President) assigned his former aide Aziz Tamba (now in prison) to buy the taxi Benzes for him. The whole idea was to be able to blend in among the public. The Head of State said he wants us to be discrete in our operations by blending with the other cab drivers in the streets. The three Benz taxis he bought for us was a mere decoy aimed at preventing the civilian population from noticing those behind the wheels. These are the taxis that we used to carry out murders, abductions, tortures, and arson attacks in the country under the President's directives," the self confessed killer alleged.

"Shortly after parking the Benz taxis at the President's Kanifing warehouse, we boarded our regular patrol vehicles, and headed for our base in Kanilai, the President's home villa. Upon our arrival at Kampfenda, a village situated at the intersection of Kanilai, we had a brief stop there, where we handed the double barrel guns to one Bobo Manga. Mr. Manga is a local hunter. He also claims to be a Marabout. He works at the President's farm," the soldier further alleged.

Upon return to their base in Kanilai, our source alleged that the President was informed that the mission to kill Deyda Hydara, has been accomplished. Assassin team leader Captain Tumbul Tamba reported to

Jammeh that the murder mission has been accomplished as instructed, the source further alleged. Mr. Tamba, and his assassin team regrouped and threw a party the next day. The dictator allegedly compensated them for their role in taking the life of journalist Deyda Hydara.

For the first time since the murder of Gambia's leading journalist Deyda Hydara, a former close confidant of President Yahya Jammeh is coming on record to shed light on the journalist's murder. Army Lance Corporal Musa Sarr, a former member of President Jammeh's Special Forces Unit stationed in Kanilai, said he was informed by his colleagues, who are members of Mr. Jammeh's assassin team that the President personally allegedly ordered for the killing of Mr. Hydara in December of 2004.

Mr. Sarr is on exile in neighboring Senegal, where he spoke to Freedom Radio on Monday, for over an hour long interview exposing the secret killings perpetrated under dictator Jammeh's eighteen years rule. Mr. Sarr spoke eloquently and confidently on a wide range of unresolved murders that occurred during dictator Jammeh's watch.

Mr. Sarr's job in Kanilai was to patrol the Gambia/Senegalese border. He said he was not part of the assassin team formed by the President Yahya Jammeh, but was privy to the activities of the group. Mr. Sarr had a cordial working relationship with the assassin team headed by Major Sanna Manjang. RSM Malick Jatta, another relegated member of the assassin team was his close buddy in the army. Sarr and Jatta normally hangout, exercise together, and in some occasions he will spend weekend with Malick Jatta at his native village Tujereng. Mr. Jatta being a central figure in Jammeh's alleged assassin team avails Sarr with the opportunity to know a lot about the activities of the unit.

Mr. Sarr was informed by one O2 Modou Jarju, alias Rambo, a member of President Jammeh's assassin team about the soldiers behind journalist Hydara's murder. Mr. Modou Jarju is a native of Kombo Brikama. Sarr said Jarju informed him that his own cousin the late Staff Sergeant Malafi Corr, Colonel Kawsu Camara, Malick Jatta, Sanna Manjang, Borra Colley, Jarju himself and others murdered Mr. Hydara. He said Modou Jarju drove a black pickup vehicle on the night of Hydara's murder. Jarju was under the company of his late cousin Malafi Corr when Hydara was ambushed and killed.

Mr. Sarr, a native of Nuimi, was shocked to learn that his cousin Malifi Corr participated in the murder of Hydara. Corr, he said, was executed back in March of 2006, alongside with Gambia's former spy chief Daba Marena, Lieutenant Ebou Lowe, RSM Alpha Bah, and co, following an abortive coup led by the erstwhile Army Chief of Defense Staf (CDS) Colonel Ndure Cham.

Musa Sarr's life began to change dramatically shortly after he learned about the massacre of his cousin Malafi Corr. He was admitted in hospital when men led by Sanna Manjang, Malick Jatta and others killed Malafi Corr, Daba Marena and others.

The government of Yahya Jammeh had earlier claimed in a press release that Corr and others escaped while being escorted to a jailhouse in Janjangbureh. But Musa Sarr said the regime's story on the fate of the detainees was a fat lie. He said Sanna Manjang, the leader of the assassin team and his friend Malick Jatta told him that Malafi Corr and co were brutally massacred. Initial attempts to kill Mr. Corr through close range gunshot failed. The assassin team resorted to massacring him, Mr. Sarr tells the Freedom Newspaper.

Mr. Sarr went on to explain an encounter he had with Solo Bojang, another member of the President's assassin team. "While stationed in Kanilai, the President's home village, my job was to patrol the Casamance/Gambia border. I remember opening fire at Solo Bojang after he ran a stop sign while we were on duty. We ordered him to stop and he refused to stop. I then open fire at him. At the time, I was very mad at the system because of the brutal murder of my cousin Malafu Corr. He was executed by Sanna Manjang and his group. I was told that Mr. Corr, Daba Marena and co were gruesomely murdered," said Musa Sarr, who fled the Gambia after he was involved in a car wreck that killed some passengers.

Sarr said he was on his way to Tujereng to deliver a consignment of marijuana on behalf of his boss Sanna Manjang to one of Manjang's drug clients, when he was involved in a car wreck. He said Manjang is in the business of supplying MFDC rebels with arms in exchange for marijuana. He recalled an instance in which Mr. Manjang had stolen a rocket launcher from the Kanilai armory and traded it to the MFDC rebels led by Salifu Sarjo for cannabis. He said Majang had close ties with the rebels.

During their patrols along the border, Manjang will ask them to wait for him and he Manjang will drive to the rebel camp to buy cannabis from the MFDC rebels. Mr. Sarr said the MFDC is using the Gambia as a safe haven to wage havoc in neighboring Senegal.

"There was this operation in which we arrested about thirty five rebels who sought refuge in the Gambia after waging a brutal attack against the Senegalese forces and communities, only to be instructed by the President to free the rebels. He asked us to escort the rebels back to the border. We caught rebels driving a Gambian vehicle, bearing the country's registration number, and insurance, in Sebanorr, guess what? After the men were processed and handed to the NIA, the President ordered for their release. Rebels organized baby naming ceremony in the Fonis. I mean inside the Gambia. It reached a time that we thought that it is a waste of time arresting the MFDC rebels since they got the President's back. We waived at them each time we spotted them within the Gambian territory," Sarr said. Mr. Sarr also said he met the leader of the MFDC Salifu Sarjo in Kanilai while Sarjo was there to meet with the President. Sarr said as long as Jammeh is the President of the Gambia it would be difficult to end the Casamance rebellion. He accuses Jammeh of backing the rebels.

Narrating how President Jammeh uses the assassin team to kill perceived Gambian political opponents and suspected witches, Sarr said while in Kanilai, a word came in that the President ordered the assassin team to murder one Mr. Ceesay of Bujulu village. Mr. Ceesay works as a watchman in one of the schools in his locality. Solo Bojang was assigned to look for Ceesay in the school with the possibilities of abducting and killing him.

The President, he said, made them to believe that Ceesay was going to be next leader of witches in the Gambia. He ordered the assassin team to kill Ceesay, he said.

"Solo Bojang led that operation. Mr. Ceesay was strangulated to death after the assassin team tied a rope on his neck," Sarr alleged. Over one thousand suspected Gambian witches were arrested and forced to drink poisonous liquids in that incident. The suspected witches were blamed for the death of the President's aunty. Many died due to poison related illnesses.

Mr. Sarr said Major Sanna Manjang, and other members of the assassin team led a team of Guinean witch hunters hired by the President to force suspected witches and wizards to drink spiritual liquids, which resulted in the death of some of the detainees. He said some of the suspected female witches were allegedly raped by Manjang and his group.

"Based on what I saw, Manjang and his group stripped off the women naked and started administering the spiritual spell on them. Some of the women were given the option to have sex with Manjang and his group or risked being forced to drink the poisonous liquid. I found packets of condoms scattered in the area in Kanilai, where the female detainees were being processed by Manjang and his group. Male folks were also stripped off naked," he said.

Mr. Sarr also commented on the killing of the forty Ghanaians in the Gambia. He said his friend Malick Jatta told him that the President ordered them to kill the Ghanaians, who were mistaken as mercenaries back in July of 2005. He said Mr. Jatta also informed him that General Borra Colley nearly messes up the operation, as one of the Ghanaian detainees attempted to escape while being escorted to the execution site. The Ghanaian was later apprehended, he said.

According to Sarr, there is a division among Jammeh's assassination team. Malick Jatta, for example, had complained to him of being unfairly "rewarded" by the President—despite executing numerous assassination missions on behalf of the President. Malick Jatta was not happy that Sanna Manjang was promoted ahead of him to the rank of

Captain, and later Major. He said Jatta repeatedly cursed out Manjang in his presence, and lamented about his inexperience in carrying out killing missions. Mr. Sarr said Malick Jatta complained to him that the President was favoring Sanna Manjang and Borra Colley in terms of promotions. Mr. Jatta thought that he was more qualified and competent than Manjang and Colley. Malick Jatta has since left the assassin team. He now works at the State House as a Regimental Sergeant Major, Sarr said.

The former head of the assassin team Colonel Kawsu Camara too was also undermined by Sollo Bojang. Sarr said since Bombaredeh is not a Jolla, Sollo Bojang saw it as an opportunity to undermine him. He said Bombaredeh had carried out many assassination missions on behalf of the President, but that did not stop Jammeh from jailing him. Sarr said it is only in the Gambia that the head of the Presidential guards can be sacked without the army rebelling. He said Bombaredeh's sacking was instigated by Sollo Bojang. He added that Bombaredeh personally told him that Sollo Bojang blocked his promotion when he was recommended to be promoted.

Regarding his working relation with Jammeh, Sarr said the President occasionally teased him because he is a Sierre. He said Jammeh onetime confronted him asking why he never smile at him during his late evening conversations with the assassin team. He told the President that he was there to do a work, and that he takes his job very seriously. He said Jammeh always wanted to maintain an eye contact with him each time he met the President.

Mr. Sarr said the assassin team is usually "wasted" (dead drunken) before embarking on the secret assassinations. He said one Alieu Jeng, a member of the assassin team nearly went mad after the massacre of the Ghanaians. He said when Sanna Manjang, Malick Jatta, and co are drunk they talked about people they assassinated on behalf of the President. The group is directly answerable to the President Yahya Jammeh, he said. He said the Army Chief of Staff has no authority, or control over the assassin team. The group only takes orders from Jammeh and no one else, he added. It is a widely feared group, Mr. Sarr tells the Freedom Newspaper.

Sarr said the late Sergeant Ello Gina Jallow, and Mustapha Colley were killed by Manjang and his group. He said Mr. Jammeh worships idols and is in the business of sacrificing human beings. He said he was informed that Ello Jallow was murdered, following allegations that he was sleeping with the President's wife.

Mr. Sarr is a trained Commando. He was trained by the Iranians, who were stationed in the Gambia to help train Jammeh's guards. He said the Iranians supplied arms to President Jammeh on numerous occasions. He talked about an underground armory built in Kanilai opposite the President's room by the Iranians. The armory is equipped with dangerous weapons, he said.

Mr. Sarr said the 13 container arms shipment that was intercepted in Nigeria by Custom officials belongs to President Jammeh. He said this was not the first time that President Jammeh has been importing arms from Iran.

"I have witnessed Iranian arms being transported into Kanilai. The Iranians trained me in Kanilai. I received a Commando certificate from the Iranian team, who were in the country to train us. If the President is telling the world that he never imported arms from Iran, that is a lie. He is not telling the truth. Almost all the arms in that armory in Kanilai came from Iran," Sarr said.

Mr. Sarr said he needs support to wage guerilla warfare against Jammeh's regime. He added that dictator Jammeh must be stopped from destroying the country by any means necessary. He said Jammeh's senseless killing of innocent Gambians got to be stopped. "If it is bravery, he is not braver than us. He is not man enough than us. I am ready to put my life on the line to bail out Gambia from Jammeh's terror," he said.

CHAPTER TWO

RSM MALICK JATTA'S REACTS TO ALLEGATIONS THAT HE IS AN ASSASSIN FOR JAMMEH

On Tuesday August 28, the Freedom Newspaper Editor embarked on an undercover operation during his radio show by posing as a former village mate of Malick Jatta, the soldier, who has been accused of allegedly killing the late Gambian journalist Deyda Hydara. The Freedom Editor phoned Regimental Sergeant Major (RSM) Malick Jatta at the beginning of his show and introduced himself to him. Mr. Jatta asked him to identify himself, which he did. Editor M'Bai began his line of conversation with Mr. Jatta by telling Malick that they grew up together in Tujereng. And that he the Editor was disturbed by reports he heard in Gambian communities linking Jatta to the alleged killing of Deyda Hydara, Dawda Nyassi, and the failed assassination attempt on the life of Gambian Lawyer Ousman Sillah. This Editor also put it to Malick Jatta that he (Malick) alongside with Lieutenant Sanna Manjang allegedly killed Hydara. He also described to Mr. Jatta how Hydara was ambushed and killed. He informed RSM Jatta that Sanna Manjang fired at Hydara at a close range, while Malick Jatta's shots killed Hydara.

Mr. Jatta reacted angrily when confronted with the said allegations. He repeatedly cursed the mother of this author. But I was able to maintain my composure since my goal was to elicit information from an alleged secret assassin allegedly hired by the Gambian dictator to harm his own people. The entire Freedom Radio audience was shocked by Jatta's repeated insults at my person and parents. Mr. Jatta insisted that before he will volunteer any information on the phone, I must reveal my source of information to him. I refused to disclose my sources to him by telling him that he Malick will harm them once their name(s) were disclosed. He then said to me in the local Mandinka dialect: "Shut the hell up if you don't want to tell me who my accusers are. I will fuck your mother if you keep calling me without telling me who these people are. I mean my accusers. Why calling me from an unknown number? I am not in for this type of mother fucking game, okay . . . Why calling me telling me things that I am not aware of? If you tell me who my accusers are, then I will be honest with you and tell you what I know."

I phoned Mr. Jatta via Skype. The self confessed assassin team member provided me with his number. I was not the least expecting a pleasant conversation from an alleged secret killer. The pertinent issues I raised during our conversation with Malick Jatta angered him. Malick Jatta could not withstand my line of questioning.

Jatta's reaction to the allegations was kind of guilt. He said once this Editor furnishes him with the names of his accuser(s), he will come out clean and tell me his own side of the story. He even calls me "my brother" during the conversation we had over the phone. Mr. Jatta repeatedly tried to persuade me to disclose my sources to him, but I refused.

During my opening remarks, I told Mr. Jatta that he was a "small boy" when I left Tujereng for America. He keenly listened to me at some point of the conversation. Mr. Jatta said getting the names of his accusers was more important to him by saying: "I will be safer if I know the people accusing me. My brother, are you not a Muslim? If I am your guy, then you should tell me who are these people accusing me. Please tell me who gave you the information. I want to know who gave you the information that I killed Hydara."

In order to win Malick Jatta's confidence, I tried to find out from him how his brother Baboucarr Jatta, the former Chief of Defense Staff of the Gambia Armed Forces was doing. I also told him that he came from a very good family. That I was shocked to learn that he (Malick) has been transformed as an alleged killer for dictator Jammeh.

Mr. Jatta kept bragging about his rank as a Regimental Sergeant Major entrusted with the Jammeh State House. He shouted at the top of his voice—urging me to be man enough to name his accusers or otherwise he will hang up the phone. He said he was ready to die for his country and go to heaven in the course of defending his Commander-in-Chief Yahya Jammeh. Malick even dares branded us as "unpatriotic citizens," residing in the West tarnishing the image of the country. The conversation was characterized by repeated insults directed at my person. I still maintain my composure.

At some point of the conversation, Malick felt comfortable. He tried to win my confidence by saying that if I am willing to help him with information about his accusers he will come out clean. He confirmed to me at some point during our conversation that there is an assassin team in the Gambia, but he was quick to say that "I am not part of that group."

He was relegated after he was accused of allegedly killing Deyda Hydara, Dawda Nyassi, and other crimes known and unknown to Gambians. Malick now works at the State House as RSM. He has left the black, black boys who are stationed in Kanilai, the President's home village, our source alleged.

When I mentioned Ousman Sonko's name as an alleged accomplice in the murder of Hydara, Malick Jatta was down for a minute. He appeared worried as to who was talking to me about a matter that was known to few in the country. "What do you say about Ousman Sonko? He asked. I put it to him that Ousman Sonko allegedly followed Mr. Hydara from the Point on his way home on the night of his assassination. That Mr. Sonko was the one updating them on the phone about Hydara's driving directions, while they were driving in two different yellow Benz taxis owned by President Jammeh.

Upon hearing such revelations, Mr. Jatta started cursing me again. He insisted that I must disclose my source to him, which I emphatically refused. I told him that he has scared the hell out of me by cursing and threatening me. Malick then decided to tone down his temper by saying: "I am not threatening you. Please speak to me. I just want you to tell me who informed you that I was the one who killed Hydara."

My identity was also a concern to Malick Jatta. He kept asking me my name throughout the conversation. At some point, I told him that my common name is MP. I also told him that I was his elder in the village. That he Malick was pretty young when I left the Gambia for the United States. He became suspicious when I told him that I was residing in the US. He went off on me at this time saying: "I know you very well."

Malick disclosed to me that our paper reported that he was involved in an incident in the Gambia some years ago, while he was in fact on mission somewhere in Africa. He said he had to download the report and show it to his Commander in Banjul.

The NIA is now reporting that two of its agents have been arrested and detained due to the Freedom Editor's conversation with RSM Malick Jatta. The wife of Ebrima Bamba Manneh, the former NIA Director, who headed the investigations into Deyda's death, was also arrested. Malick Jatta is claiming that the NIA is the main source of the Freedom Newspaper story.

Prior to speaking with Malick Jatta, our source informed us that the best way to penetrate Jatta's co alleged assassin team member Sanna Manjang, was to use a lady to phone him. Our source said Mr. Manjang enjoys the company of ladies. That a lady can make him to talk about issues that he (Manjang) wouldn't want to discuss one and one basis with a male folk. Couples of phone calls were placed on Manjang's cellular phone, but all the calls went on voicemail. Mr. Manjag's own side of the story on the damning allegations could not be obtained.

Captain Tumbul Tamba, who allegedly took part in the murder Hydara, died years later under mysteriously circumstances. He was briefly admitted in hospital before dying of stomach pain. Major Musa Jammeh too died under similar circumstances. General Borra Colley, another alleged Jammeh assassin team member, and also the Director General of Gambia's Prison Department has been placed on sick leave due to major health issues. Borra has not been reporting to work for months now.

Based on an interview I had with one of Jammeh's alleged assassin team members, the following security personnel are on the dictator's assassin payroll. Please note that some of the soldiers and officers mentioned below have been promoted, or sacked prior to the interview I had with the alleged Jammeh assassin team member.

Major General Saul Badjie
General Bora Colley
Colonel Solo Bojang
Major Sana Manjang
Major Nuha Badjie
Captain Modou Jarju
Wo1 Malick Jatta
O2 Michael Correa
02 Fansu Nyabally
WO2 Bai Lowe
Ex Colonel Kawsu Camara
O2 Mustapha Sanneh
O2 Michael Jatta
02 Alieu Jeng
Captain Landing Tamba
Captain Salifu Corr
02 Musa Badjie

Below is the list of the reinforcement team that serves as a backup for Jammeh's assassin team:

John K Mendy
Momodou Lamin Tamba (now dismissed)
Sang Mendy
Staff Sergeant Abdoulie Jallow
Staff Sergeant Malick Manga
Sergeant Sulayman Sambou

The above mentioned soldiers and officers of the Gambia Armed Forces are part of dictator Yahya Jammeh's alleged killing machine in Banjul. These are the folks who allegedly hide under the cover of darkness to fire bomb newspaper houses, radio stations critical of the regime, and occasionally kill journalists and perceived political opponents in the Gambia. The same group allegedly burnt down Radio One FM, which left its proprietor George Christensen to suffer high degree burns, and the failed assassination attempt on the life of lawyer Ousman Sillah.

During the criminal trial of the late House Majority Leader Baba Kajali Jobe, who was jailed for nine years on economic crime related charges, dictator Jammeh allegedly instructed his assassin team to kill Baba Jobe, and his defense team. Mr. Jobe was represented by a renowned Gambian criminal trial lawyer Ousman Sillah and Mai Fatty. Both Lawyers properly represented Jobe during his trial.

Mr. Jammeh was unhappy with some of the revelations coming from the court, our source alleged. He accused Mr. Jobe of Tax evasion, and also embezzling the Youth Development Enterprise Funds (YDE). Jammeh owns YDE. Businesses affiliated with Jammeh are usually exempted from paying taxes. Jobe's trial was politically motivated. Jammeh threw Jobe under bus after using him against the Gambian people, a former associate of Baba Jobe has alleged.

According to a member of Jammeh's alleged assassin team, the President allegedly assigned them during the trial of Baba Jobe to ambush and kill Lawyer Ousman Sillah. Mr. Sillah was coming from a wedding ceremony, when he was shot at a close range by Sanna Manjang, while he was about to park his car at his home. He was driving a red car at the time of the incident.

This author was among the local journalists, who visited Mr. Sillah's home shortly after the shooting incident, which prompted Sillah's immediate evacuation to Senegal for treatment. At the scene of the failed assassination attempt, one could see battered car window glasses scattered next to Ousman Sillah's compound gate. There were blood stains visible on the floor and inside the car.

The alleged Jammeh hired killer interviewed by this author said they thought that Mr. Sillah was dead when Mr. Manjang open fire on him. Mr. Borra Colley, also an alleged assassin for Jammeh walked near Mr. Sillah's car window to check if he was dead. Mr. Colley was supposed to finish Mr. Sillah with another shot, but he thought that Sillah was dead, our source alleged.

"Pa, to kill a human being is not easy. We all thought that Ousman Sillah was dead when Sanna Manjang opens fire at him. On the whole, he pretended like if he was dead, when he was actually alive. He faked his death. The plan was: Borra was supposed to fire the last shot to finish him, but he never bothered to open fire at him," our source alleged. The hit man confessed to me that they were driving a van when they attempted on the life of Ousman Sillah.

Major General Saul Badjie was on the ground on the day in question, he alleged. Saul Badjie falsified his credentials when he joined the Gambia National Army. His real name is Karafa Bojang, and not Saul Badjie. He is from Bwiam. He had secondary education. There used to be one Sulayman, a former graduate of the Saint Augustine's High school, he grew up with in Bwiam. Saul and Karafa Bojang, now AKA Saul Badjie grew up in Bwiam. It's not clear if Saul Badjie stole his school certificate to join the army, but what is clear though is that Saul Badjie was not a promising student in school.

Jammeh's reaction to Ousman Sillah's failed assassination attempt during a Legal Year address was: "My soldiers are well trained. They are professionals. If they were indeed involved in the shooting of Ousman Sillah, they will never shoot and miss a target." But the Jammeh alleged assassin team member disagrees. He said the President allegedly ordered them to kill Ousman Sillah, and that Sanna Manjang fired the shots that rendered Sillah unconscious.

Mr. Sillah was briefly hospitalized at the Ndemban Clinic, before he was flown to Dakar, Senegal for further medical attention. He later resettled in Raleigh, North Carolina, in the United States of America, where he lived for some years before his home return to the Gambia.

According to our source, Lawyer Mai Fatty too was also on their radar for assassination. He said the President has given them directives to allegedly kill Mr. Fatty, but luckily for him, Fatty left the country after he survived from an auto mobile accident. He said Mr. Fatty was placed on close surveillance during the trial of Baba Jobe.

"We laid an ambush for Baba Jobe for days on the Soma/Banjul Highway. The plan was to attack his vehicle and possibly kill him. But the day he passes through the road, we were in Kanilai to take bath. We later learned that Baba had crossed and was heading for the Kombos. The President was very upset when the news was relayed to him. He wanted Ousman Sillah, Mai Fatty, and Baba Jobe dead," said the self confessed Jammeh hit man alleged.

The hitman also informed me that back in 2004, the Gambian dictator allegedly issued a list of Gambians to be murdered by his alleged assassin team. The list contained the names of over twenty perceived political opponents. Journalists, Lawyers and human rights activists dominated the list. My name featured on the list of Gambians targeted to be murdered allegedly by the dictator, according to the self confessed killer.

Major Kalifa Bajinka, the former Kanilai Camp Commander saved my life, he claimed. He described Major Bajinka as a God fearing Muslim, who refuses to execute the dictator's alleged orders when the list of the targeted assassinations was brought to Bajinka's attention. Major Bajinka at the time was in charge of soldiers stationed in Kanilai.

"Pa, Major Bajinka is a good man. He has saved the lives of many Gambians while in Kanilai as a Camp Commander. I remember the President instructing him to coordinate the list of over twenty Gambians that Mr. Jammeh lined up to be assassinated, but Mr. Bajinka refused to enforce the order. He has always advised us not to kill any Gambian. Your name was on that list of Gambians to be murdered," he alleged.

According to a former close aide of President Jammeh, Mr. Bajinka phoned the late Journalist Deyda Hydara, few days before his murder informing him about the plot that was hatched for his possible murder.

The source said Mr. Hydara was advised by Major Bajinka to leave the country if he could because a plot was hatched for his murder. Mr. Hydara, known for his fearlessness refused to be intimidated. He was quoted as saying that he was ready to die for the country in the execution of his duty as a journalist. Our source said Major Bajinka nearly had problems with Ousman Sonko and the late Tumbul Tamba, following his private conversation with Hydara. He was later moved from Kanilai to another unit in the army.

Major Bajinka and President Jammeh parted company shortly after his return from a military training in Nigeria in 2006. He was alleged to have been implicated in a coup plot led by the former Army Chief of Defense Staff Colonel Ndure Cham. Mr. Bajinka has denied his involvement in any coup attempt. He refused to submit himself to NIA arrest, when some agents of the National Intelligence Agency showed up at his residence to pick him up for questioning. He was armed at the time, and reports have it that Major Bajinka issued some warning shots instructing the NIA agents to leave his residence. Bajinka later fled to neighboring Senegal, before a military backup team was dispatched to arrest him. Mr. Bajinka is currently residing in the United States of America with his family. Mr. Bajinka used to be one of the longest serving ADCS attached to the Gambian despot. He was very close to Jammeh.

CHAPTER THREE

DAWDA NYASSI MURDERED

Dawda Nyassi is a native of Foni Bondali. He was sitting home with his family in Bakoteh, when his friend one Mr. Gibba invited him to meet with him at the Bakoteh "Bantaba." Mr. Gibba at the time had allegedly conspired with the late Tumbul Tamba, a former army Captain, allegedly heading President Jammeh's assassin team to help facilitate the abduction of Dawda Nyassi. The agreement that was allegedly reached between Tumbul and Gibba was that both Gibba and Nyassi will be picked up by the security agents, and while on their way to the execution site situated around the fence of the Banjul International Airport, Gibba will be dropped somewhere around the Talinding Market.

Mr. Nyassi used to be a former rebel in Liberia. He was among the mercenaries who allegedly participated in the Liberian war. He later returned to the Gambia, where he resided until his secret abduction and murder. Mr. Nyassi suffered numerous arrests in the hands of the National Intelligence Agency, the (NIA) prior to his killing.

The Gambian leader never trusted Nyassi, our source alleged. And as such, he instructed his alleged assassin team to put him on watch list. There were occasions in the past Mr. Nyassi disappeared from his family, and later released from state custody. No reason was advanced for his secret abductions.

While Mr. Nyassi and his friend Gibba were chatting at the Bakoteh Bantaba, a tainted Mitsubishi pickup truck with registration number:

BJL 1074 arrived. Both men were manhandled and dumped into the waiting truck. One Lamin Jarju, a soldier was the driver of the vehicle at the time.

As the assassin team reached the Talinding Market, Mr. Gibba, who allegedly "setup" his friend Dawda Nyassi to be abducted and killed by Jammeh's alleged hit men, was asked to disembark from the vehicle. Captain Tumbul Tamba and his men speeded towards the Banjul International Airport.

Upon arrival at the execution site, which is close to the airport fence, Mr. Dawda Nyass was tied on a tree and shot at a close range by Major Sanna Manjang, RSM Malick Jatta, and one Alieu Jeng, alias Alieu Njie, our source alleged. Mr. Jeng is a native of Banjul.

After killing Nyassi, they dug a hole and buried his remains near a tree. During this time, Captain Tumbul Tamba, Lamin Jarju, and Bai Lowe, both drivers assigned to the alleged assassin team were sitting quietly watching the unfolding execution of Dawda Nyassi.

Mr. Nyassi was taken aback by the developments. He never anticipated that his own friend will set him up for a murder, our source alleged. He was kind of speechless for a minute. He doesn't know what might have necessitated his abduction and execution.

Looking confused, and worried, Mr. Nyassi could be heard asking his executioners: "What have I done to warrant my killing? What have I done? I left Liberia and return to my home country, and yet I am not given peace of mind. Why do you have to kill me? Please spare my life."

Mr. Nyassi's passionate pleas to be forgiven by the President's alleged hit men did not stop them from killing him. He was murdered and his remains dumped into a hole next to a tree very close to the airport fence. Tumbul Tamba later reported to Jammeh that the mission to kill Dawda Nyassi has been accomplished, the self confessed Jammeh hit man alleged.

Like Dawda Nyassi, the former Daily Observer Sub-Editor Ebrima Chief Manneh, was arrested from work by some security agents. His arrest was allegedly instigated by the President. There were conflicting reports associated with Manneh's arrest. One report suggested that he was caught by Pa Malick Faye, the Managing Director of the Observer Company downloading a BBC story critical of President Jammeh during the African Union Summit that was held in Banjul, while another report suggests that Chief's arrest might have to do with his affiliation with Gambia's former spy chief Daba Marena, who was implicated in the March 2006 coup attempt.

Chief Manneh died while in state custody. His remains were dumped in a well in Kanilai, the President's home village, our source alleged. The late Daba Marena, Lieutenant Ebou Lowe, Malafi Corr, RSM Alpha Bah, and other missing political inmates were also allegedly dumped in the same well. Sanna Manjang dropped his pistol into the well while they were dumping the bodies of Marena and co, our source alleged.

It is important to note that after killing Daba Marena and co, the government came up with a press release claiming that the inmates escaped from custody while the vehicle they were travelling with to a jailhouse in Janjangbureh crashes. Since then no one heard from the inmates. It was apparent that they were killed by the regime. This was confirmed by Jammeh's alleged assassin team member. He said he witnessed the execution of Daba Marena and co.

Since assuming the mantle of leadership in the Gambia, Mr. Jammeh has been accused of killing a good number of coup suspects without availing them with the opportunity of due process before the law. The massacre of the November 11, 1994 coup suspects is still fresh in the minds of Gambians.

Mr. Jammeh has also been accused of murdering fourteen Gambian students who protested against the killing of their colleague one Ebrima Barry, who was tortured to death by the personnel of the Brikama Fire and Ambulance Services. Dozens of other students were maimed in that incident.

A newly born Gambian baby, who was dumped by her mum immediately after labor, and was "adopted" by Gambia's First Lady Zeinab Suma Jammeh back in 2000, has disappeared—amid speculations that the dictator might have allegedly sacrificed the girl as a ritual. The baby was being taken care of by a foster parent at the Bakoteh Children's village, where the First Lady offered to adopt the baby as her parent. At the time, her daughter baby Mariam Jammeh needed a company, and she thought that the best way to keep her child entertained was to become a foster parent.

Zeinab left the State House under the company of Fatou Jahoumpa Ceesay, Nyimasata Sanneh Bojang, and a handful of her protocol staff to the Children's village to ask the SOS management to help allow her adopt the abandoned new born baby. Management agreed, and she later showed up with a pregnant goat, bag of rice, cooking oil and Cola-nut to christen the baby.

The SOS staff, including the foster parents at the SOS threw a party for the child. The baby was named after the President's wife Zeinab Souma Jammeh. The goat that was brought by Zeinab died, when a heavy storm hit the SOS village, a source said.

Fatou Jahoumpa Ceesay, and Nyimasata Sanneh Bojang played a crucial role towards the baby's adoption. Nyimasata used to work with the SOS as a Social case worker prior to joining the Jammeh regime. She was very familiar with the SOS.

The First Lady came to pick up the child a month after the naming ceremony. She told the girl's foster parent that she was going to take her to the State House to keep her daughter accompany. There is nothing wrong with Zeinab adopting an abandoned kid, but the circumstances surrounding the child adoption raises a red flag. There was no legal paperwork signed to account for the adopted child.

For eleven solid years, the SOS adopted child is nowhere to be seen around Zeinab's kids. The baby was last seen by the SOS management when Zeinab, FJC and Nyimasata Sanneh Bojang came to adopt her.

Concerned parties approached the Freedom Newspaper asking for help to locate the adopted SOS girl. The parties concerned said they were present when the First Lady was accompanied by Fatou Jahoumpa Ceesay, and Nyimasata Sanneh Bojang asking the SOS Management for the baby to be adopted by Zeinab.

During our investigations, we interviewed numerous sources within the Jammeh State House. One insider said he was aware of the child adoption. The insider said after adopting the child, the First Lady decided to give the baby to her aunty one Hadija. Hadija raised Zeinab when she was poor child. She has not been blessed with a child in her lifetime, the insider said.

According to the State House insider, the baby was never hosted at the State House, contrary to Zeinab's initial impression that she was going to raise her with Mariam. The baby was staying with Hadija at a property within the Greater Banjul Area, the insider tells the Freedom Newspaper. He said Hadija will occasionally bring the baby to the State House to interact with baby Mariam. "The baby later stopped coming to the State House. I don't know where she is right now. I don't know whether she is alive, or has been sacrificed by the President," the insider said.

"I do know for a fact that the President worships idols. He has "Jalangs" in Kanilai. One Faye Bojang has been assigned by Jammeh to pour alcohol on the "Jalangs" on every Thursday and Friday. This has been a routine practice. Even whereas the President is away, Faye Bojang must pour alcohol on the Jallangs. The President worships idols," the source said.

Captain Mahmoud Babadi Sarr, was at his home relaxing after closing from work, when officers of Gambia's National Intelligence Agency came to pick him up for questioning back in 2009. He notified his family about his NIA encounter before he was taken away. Mr. Sarr, who goes with the aliases MB Sarr, has been missing for the past three years. Mr. Sarr used to be the commander of Gambia's Navy. He has been under government custody without any formal criminal charges filed against him.

Mr. Sarr's disappearance received no media attention. His case is known to very few people in the Gambia. Sarr is a reserved gentleman. He goes to work, come back home and take care of his family life, as every responsible family head will do. He was not into politics at all. He was one of Gambia's most professional army officers.

Mr. Sarr grew up in Sierra Leone, where he attended higher education before he returned to his native country the Gambia. He later joined the Gambia National Army. His specialization was the Marine—known as the Gambia Navy. He worked with the likes of the former junta Spokesman Ebou Jallow.

Mr. Sarr is related to the Sarr family in Kent Street in Banjul. Part of his family also lives in Macdonald Street. His wife is a Sierra Leonean. He left his kids behind, while he continually tumbles in prison without knowing why he is in jail in the first place. His wife and other family members are helping to take care of his kids while his fate in prison remains uncertain.

Mr. Sarr's family do not seems to know about his whereabouts. They last saw Mr. Sarr, when security agents acting under the directives of the country's iron fist dictator President Yahya Jammeh came for him. He has since been missing. No one in his family contacted seems to know where Mr. Sarr has been detained.

The Freedom Newspaper conducted an investigation into MB Sarr's case and found that the former naval chief is held at the state central prison in Banjul. Mr. Sarr has not been told as to why he is still in jail—beside what the NIA told him that the President personally ordered for his arrest.

Like MB Sarr, many Gambians have gone missing under such circumstances. Many enforced disappearances are allegedly spearheaded by the Head of State himself. Mr. Jammeh will just wake up one morning and said I want Mr. X, or Z disappeared and his operatives will enforce his directives. Sarr's case though is unique due to his Sierra Leonean ties.

This is not the first time that Mr. Sarr has disappeared from his family. He has been detained on three different occasions. One of his arrests has to do with allegations of Sarr being allegedly complicit to a failed coup plot back in March of 2006. He has denied such allegations. But his last arrest is causing nightmare for his family. The family has been denied access to the detainee. On top of that, the regime in Banjul is not coming up with any information about MB Sarr's whereabouts.

Besides being a Naval Chief, Mr. Sarr was also a successful businessman in Banjul. It is not clear if the dictator targeted him due to his business success story. The Kanilai monster doesn't want to see a genuine competitor in the business market. He occasionally annexes people's business firms into his growing business empire.

MB Sarr is a prisoner of conscience. Amnesty International, Human Right Watch, the United Nations, and other rights groups should include Mr. Sarr on their list of missing Gambians. Mr. Sarr was illegally kidnapped from his family. Dictator Jammeh should be held responsible if anything happen to MB Sarr.

Mr. Sarr has always been known as a perfect gentleman. We implore on all peace loving Gambians to join us in condemning Sarr's false imprisonment and kidnapping. The Kanilai monster's terror against our people has no boundary. He is going after decent Gambians such as MB Sarr, who lived their life with honesty, prestige, and humility. We demand for MB Sarr's unconditional release!

Back in July of 2005, while Mr. Jammeh and his party supporters were celebrating the military revolution that brought him to power, a word came in from his former Inspector General of police Ousman Sonko, who informed Mr. Jammeh about the arrest of some West African suspected mercenaries, who were rounded up in Barra. Mr. Jammeh's reaction to the news of the Immigrant's detention was: "kill them all," our source alleged.

Mr. Musa Mboob was the Director General of Gambia's Immigration Department at the time of the mass execution of the suspected West African mercenaries. Mr. Mboob told me in an interview on September

32

11, 2012, that he was sitting with the President Yahya Jammeh at the McCarthy Square, now known as the July 22nd Square in Banjul, when Ousman Sonko, the then IGP walked pass him to inform Mr. Jammeh about the arrest of the suspected mercenaries. Mr. Mboob said the majority those arrested were Ghanaian nationals. Mr. Mboob also said the incident was brought to his attention by one Inspector Jawara, the former station officer of the Barra police station. Jawara phoned Mr. Mboob to inform Mboob that his men (the Immigration agents posted in Barra) arrested some West African nationals suspected of trying to migrate to Spain through sailing. Mr. Mboob then contacted his officers on the ground and they confirmed to him about the apprehension of the West African nationals.

The former Immigration Chief said his officers couldn't get the chance to process the detained Immigrants. Under normal circumstances, Mboob said the Immigration Department was supposed to identify all the detainees and get in touch with their respective embassies accredited to the Gambia before making a concrete decision on their case. But Musa Mboob, who now resides in the United States with his family after a short tenure serving as the Deputy Chief of Mission at the Gambian Embassy in Washington DC, said he was sidelined during the apprehension of the West African nationals. An instruction came from the Gambian President Yahya Jammeh that the detainees should be executed, he alleged. And what followed next was the mass execution of the detainees, Mr. Mboob said.

Mr. Mboob said the detainees were divided into groups and were executed in grand style by soldiers led by the late Major Musa Jammeh. The former Army Chief of Defense Staff Lang Tombong Tamba, who is now on death row, after been implicated in a failed coup in 2009, was very instrumental in the coordination of the execution of the detainees, Mr. Mboob alleged. He also stated that the former police chief Ousman Sonko, Lang Tombong, Musa Jammeh, Tumbul Tamba, Kawsu Camara, alias Bombaredeh, and others took part in the killing of the Ghanaians and other West African nationals. Close to sixty detainees were executed by the Gambian Government, he said.

"The detainees were summarily executed under the directives of the President Yahya Jammeh without been processed by my Department. Under normal circumstances, the detainees ought to have been interviewed by the Immigration Department. I mean we should have been allowed to sort them out; by finding out whether they entered this country legally; what was the purpose of them being in the country in the first place, and so on. But unfortunately, the detainees were never accorded the right to due process. They were tied in robes and taken to the execution site, where they were subjected to brutal torture before their execution. Fortunately, one of the Ghanaian detainees escaped," Musa Mboob said.

Mr. Mboob said he launched a protest with the former police chief Ousman Sonko, by expressing outrage at the killings of the non Gambians and the state's interference with the job of the Immigration Department. Mr. Mboob said the killings were not justified and it undermines international law on the processing of Immigrants intercepted in foreign countries.

The Inspector General of police Mr. Sonko allegedly informed Mr. Mboob that the orders to kill the suspected mercenaries came from the higher-ups (the President Yahya Jammeh). He also told Mr. Mboob that the matter was beyond his control.

Mr. Mboob said the murdered West African nationals were not mercenaries as claimed by the government. He said the detainees were trying to migrate to Spain in search of greener pasture, but in the process were mistaken as mercenaries by the paranoid Gambian dictator. He said Mr. Jammeh unilaterally decided to order for the execution of the detainees without putting into consideration the diplomatic implications associated with his actions.

The Jammeh regime later came under increasing scrutiny and attacks directed at the dictatorship by human rights groups, who criticized the administration for acting outside the dictates of laws of the Gambia by killing the detainees without availing them with due process. Bereaved families in Ghana also demanded justice in the case of their loved ones who were murdered in the Gambia.

The Ghanaian massacre in the Gambia later became an international issue—with both the United Nations and the Ghanaian government stepping in pressurizing the Jammeh administration to furnish them with a detailed report about the killing of the detainees.

The authorities in Banjul were also required to handover the bodies of the murdered Ghanaians to their families so that a decent burial can be accorded to them. The President Yahya Jammeh also extended monetary compensation to the affected Ghanaian families in an attempt to settle the matter out of court. The Ghanaian Government accepted Jammeh's money. It was distributed among the affected Ghanaian families.

According to one former Jammeh aide: "The former IGP Essa Badjie saved President Jammeh when the UN investigators came to collect the bodies of the murdered Ghanaians. Essa Badjie lied to the UN officials that the bodies were buried at the Jeswang cemetery, when in fact the bodies were indeed dumped in a well in Kanilai. I know where the well is situated."

"The UN team left with the Gambian dead bodies and not Ghanaians. We all know what happened on the day in question. The Ghanaians were slaughtered and dumped in a well in Kanilai. That was one of the reasons why the President has credited Essa Badjie as one of his "best IGPS" ever in the history of Gambia's police. Little did he know that some of us around him in Kanilai have been closely monitoring his crimes against humanity. The UN should understand that they took wrong bodies to Ghana," Our source alleged.

The former Immigration boss said Jammeh's leadership lacks credibility. The execution of the inmates, institutionalized corruption, and the flagrant abuse of the rights of citizens are common features in the Gambia, he alleged. He said the late Musa Jammeh confessed to him personally during a casual conversation with Musa Jammeh, who informed him that he (Musa Jammeh) shot and killed Almamo Manneh, a former close aide of President Jammeh. Mr. Manneh was accused of coup plot by the state.

"The late Major Musa Jammeh told me during a conversation I had with him before his demise that he killed Lieutenant Almamo Manneh. He said he fired the shots that killed Mr. Manneh. Musa Jammeh spoke to me freely while bragging about killing Almamo Manneh. It is sad that Musa Jammeh was transformed as an assassin for the dictator," the former police chief Musa Mboob alleged.

Almamo Manneh used to be a personal friend and also a strong loyalist of President Jammeh. He used to brag that before anyone could get to Jammeh, he would be the first person to be killed. He has always been loyal to dictator Jammeh. His loyalty to President Jammeh was evident on his frequent showcasing of military weapons that he usually carries during Presidential escorts to scare potential enemies.

Mr. Manneh ended being set up by Ousman Sonko, who called him at the middle of the night to inform him that he had a message to deliver to him from the President, one of our sources alleged. Mr. Manneh left his wife and kids to meet with Ousman Sonko, only for him to be murdered. Mr. Manneh at the time had sold his groundnut that he cultivated at his farm to President Jammeh. The President told him that he needed the peanuts so that he (Jammeh) could process it into groundnut butter. Mr. Manneh was under the impression that he was meeting with genuine colleagues—only for him to be ambushed and killed, our source explained.

The late Almamo Manneh named his son after President Jammeh. His wife is currently residing in Raleigh, North Carolina with the kids. Mr. Jammeh has allegedly rendered many Gambian families orphanage. He accused Almamo Manneh, Lieutenant Landing Sanneh and co of coup plot. Manneh was killed, while Sanneh was shot by the arresting team. One Mr. Dumbuya, a State Guard soldier was also allegedly killed by guards headed by Kawsu Camara, AKA Bombardeh. Mr. Dumbuya was chased into the Banjul Albert Market, where he was overpowered and shot to death by the State Guards.

Mr. Mboob also recalled when the former CDS Lang Tombong Tamba came to his office and allegedly solicited him to append his signature on Taiwanese checks that he (Tamba) never explains to Mboob about the main motive why he should append his signature on the checks. Mboob refused to sign the checks, and in turn phoned the Interior Minister Ousman Sonko, who pleaded with him to sign the Taiwanese checks. Mr. Sonko told Mr. Mboob that the practice of Security Chiefs signing Taiwanese checks have been in place since he (Sonko) was at the police as IGP. Mr. Mboob was still defiant. He said he refused to sign the checks since his job does not relate to processing cash for the police, the military, or the Immigration Department. He said he suspected some kind of fraud in regards to the Taiwanese checks that Mr. Tamba allegedly solicited him to sign.

According to Mr. Mboob, Lang Tombong Tamba has always developed hatred and grudges against him. He says Tamba allegedly instigated his transfer from the Immigration Department to the police, where Jammeh elevated him to the position of an Inspector General of police. Tamba and his cohorts makeup allegations that he (Mboob) has abused his office while serving as Gambia's Immigration boss, he alleged.

The original plan was to get Mr. Mboob arrested and charged, but the President told Tamba and his group that in order to build up a strong case against Mr. Mboob, he should be transferred to the police for the time being before any indictment could be proffered against him, Mr. Mboob further alleged.

Mr. Jammeh and Musa Mboob were enrolled in the National Gendarmerie the same day. Mr. Jammeh was not convinced that Mr. Mboob would indulge in activities that would put him and his office into disrepute. Mboob said his hands were clean and that he had nothing to hide.

President Jammeh invited Mr. Mboob to the State House, where he informed Mboob that he wanted him to be the country's top police chief. Mr. Jammeh also asked Mboob if he could identify someone to replace him at the Immigration Department. Jammeh told Mboob to also contact the Public Service Commission once he was done with his recruitment process so that his successor could be officially appointed.

While Mr. Mboob was busy trying to figure out who should succeed him, Jammeh personally mentioned the name of one Buba Sanyang alias Zil Sanyang, a former Immigration OC stationed at the airport. Saiko Drammeh's name also came up during his meeting with Mr. Mboob. Mr. Mboob said he was not surprised by the President's recommendation of Zil Sanyang to be part of his succession team because Zil was subordinating him during his last days at the Immigration Department. He said Zil was allegedly acting in concert with Lang Tombong Tamba and co to get him sacked and arrested.

When Mr. Mboob summoned Zil Sanyang into his office to inform him about the news of his appointment as an Immigration Deputy Director, alongside with Saiko Drammeh, who was appointed Immigration Director General, Mboob said Zil's reaction was kind of disrespectful towards him. He could read signs of insubordination on the side of Mr. Sanyang, he said. He said Mr. Sanyang downplayed his appointment, and was not keen at paying attention to what he (Mboob) was saying.

Come the Ndure Cham 2006 March abortive coup, Mr. Mboob alleged that Lang Tombong saw it as an opportunity to implicate him. He was arrested and detained for sometime before he was cleared from any wrongdoing. Mr. Mboob also said Lang Tombong Tamba could have help to save the lives of the other innocent coup suspects such as Daba Marena and co, but he failed to properly advise the President resulting to their alleged mass execution. He said Mr. Marena used to be a close friend of Lang Tombong, while he (Marena) was an NIA attaché at the State House. Mr. Marena hang out and travel with Lang overseas, Mr. Mboob said.

Three years down the road, Tamba was arrested alongside with other army chiefs accused of plotting to overthrow the administration of President Jammeh. Mr. Tamba was also accused of being a complicit in the 2006 failed coup attempt, which he later leaked to the President. He is currently on death row.

"The evil that men do, do live after them. Lang Tombong Tamba appears to be a very nice guy on a personal level, but he is very malicious and deceptive. Lang has plotted against me on numerous times in an attempt to get me into trouble, but he who God blessed, no one can curse. Lang is today suffering in jail because of his bad deeds against other people. He has implicated so many innocent people while in office. Some of his victims have been arrested, tortured, dismissed from their jobs, and others killed," Mr. Mboob alleged.

Mr. Mboob said throughout his service with the Gambian government he has never harmed, or harassed any Gambian. That was one of the reasons why when President Jammeh allegedly wanted to make his Philippine maid (secret mistress) to disappear in thin air Mboob decided to step his foot against it. Mr. Jammeh had instructed Mboob to send the lady packing with the next available flight to the Philippines. Mr. Mboob said he has registered his disapproval at any attempt to harm the lady.

The President was alleged to have been sexually socializing with his Philippine maid and when the information reached the lady's boyfriend, who was a foreign diplomat accredited to the Gambia, it further strained her relationship with Jammeh. He later allegedly ordered for the lady to be kicked out of the country empty handed.

Seriegn Modou Njie, the former State Guard Commander, together with Fatou Njie, a Protocol officer attached to the First Lady Zeinab Souma Jammeh took part in the operations to deport the Philippine Lady, Mr. Mboob said. He told me that he accompanied Serign Modou Njie and Fatou Njie to the lady's residence in Kanifing, where she was arrested and placed on deportation without any court removal hearing.

Mr. Mboob alleged that the President's original plan was to harm the Lady, but thank God he was able to process her to leave the country unharmed. There was no flight to facilitate her deportation on the day in question. Mr. Mboob said he had to personally book a hotel for the lady, and the next day she was deported to her native country.

When the President enquired from Mr. Mboob as to whether the Lady has been deported as instructed, Mr. Mboob said he answered in the affirmative. He said at time the Philippine Lady was still in the Gambia, but he had to protect her because Jammeh insisted that she must leave the country.

"I later find out that the main problem between Jammeh and his maid was due to a secret sexual relationship that transpired between the two, and it later came to the attention of the lady's boyfriend in the Gambia, a foreign diplomat. I saved that Lady's life. Jammeh wanted to harm her," Mr. Mboob alleged.

CHAPTER FOUR

JAMMEH EXECUTED FIRST BATCH OF DEATH ROW INMATES

President Yahya Jammeh last night ordered for the execution of the nine death row inmates—just hours before he replaced his Foreign Minister Mamburay Njie, who was redeployed to the Education Ministry as Minister for Higher Education. Mr. Jammeh went ahead with the executions as promised. Seven Gambian death row inmates and two Senegalese nationals who were on death row were executed in grand style, prison sources intimated. The move followed an international condemnation—denouncing dictator Jammeh's latest attempt to kill the death row inmates.

Nigerian President Jonathan Goodluck, who has been lobbying for sub-regional support to prevail on Jammeh to put on hold on the planned executions said: "Such an act would mean genocide in Africa, after that of Rwanda." Similar denunciations of Jammeh's move also came from the newly elected French President. "France therefore urges Gambia to maintain this moratorium with a view toward the definitive abolition of the death penalty, and not to execute these death row prisoners. It also demands that Gambia commute all death sentences to custodial sentences," the French President said.

There has been confusion within Jammeh's own Cabinet about the ongoing executions of the death row inmates. The President made his promise good, as he executed the first batch of the death row inmates. Foreign Minister Mamburay Njie, who was apparently opposed to the President's move tried to convince Jammeh not to carry out the killings, but Njie was immediately instructed to vacate his office. Jammeh reassigned him to a different Ministry, while he (Jammeh) was busy coordinating the executions.

The following inmates have been executed based on credible information coming from the state main prison.

Lamin Darboe
Lamin Jarju, a former army Lieutenant
Lamin F Jammeh, a former Army Lieutenant
Alieu Bah, a former army officer
Malang Sonko
Buba Yabo
Dawda Bojang
Dawda Bojang
Tambara Samba, Senegalese
Gibe Bah, Senegalese

A Freedom Newspaper source was able to speak to sources close to the Mile Two Prison, who confirmed that the executed detainees were escorted from their cells last night to be killed. The President ordered for the first batch of the death row of inmates to be executed

Prior to the executions, President Jammeh instructed the army command to return medals and cell phones belonging to his former CDS Lang Tombong Tamba, and other security detainees on death row. There was a great sign of relief among families thinking that the President was about to pardon the convicts. But a week later, Jammeh as usual surprises the nation with his planned execution of the inmates. Nine inmates have been executed so far.

Unimpeachable sources in the heart of the Jammeh administration have confirmed to the Freedom Newspaper that the nine death row inmates, whose fate attracted local and international outcry, were indeed executed through lethal injection by agents acting under the orders of the Gambian erratic leader Yaya Jammeh. The following is an account of what happened in regards to the executed inmates at the Mile Two prison according to our sources: "The inmates were taken out of their cells Thursday night to an office near the bakery in Mile Two, where they were executed by injection. The prisoners later saw them loading the bodies of the executed inmates in a vehicle and taken away."

Our knowledgeable sources witnessed what happened on the night of Thursday, and the fact that the government is denying it is false. The inmates were indeed executed through lethal injection. The international community, including Senegal should insist on the government producing the bodies of the murdered inmates so that they could be accorded a decent burial.

The leakage of the mass execution of the death row inmates was an intelligence failure on the side of the Jammeh murder machine. The dictator was allegedly under the impression that he could kill these people without anyone knowing about it, but little did he realize that inside the Mile Two prison, our informants are embedded there.

We received credible information from our sources once Jammeh's execution taskforce step their foot at the Mile Two prison. The execution was carried out through lethal injection, which is completely new to Gambians. The only execution carried out in the Gambia under Jawara's rule was done through firing by hanging.

The following inmates were killed:

1. Lamin Darboe, an inmate who served more than twenty years in prison

2. Lamin Jarju, a former army Lieutenant

3. Lamin F Jammeh, a former Army Lieutenant

4. Alieu Bah, a former army officer

5. Malang Sonko

6. Buba Yabo

7. Dawda Bojang

8. Tabara Samba, Senegalese

9. Gebe Bah, Senegalese

President Jammeh lied to President Macky Sall of Senegal when he told him on the phone that the inmates were in safe custody. Jammeh said he was merely threatening Gambians when he swore to execute the death row inmates. Macky and his team in Dakar appeared convinced by Jammeh's lies. Alieu Tin, the Human Rights activist also bought the Jammeh cheap explanation, while citing opposition sources to alley the fear of his countrymen in Senegal. Two days after the Freedom story on the execution of the inmates, Jammeh admitted that he indeed executed the nine inmates; two of whom were Senegalese nationals.

Perhaps, Macky Sall is not aware of Jammeh's pattern of lying history. Jammeh has always been a pathological liar. If Jammeh can deny killing Deyda Hydara, Koro Ceesay, Chief Manneh, Haruna Jammeh, his own brother, Jasaja Kujabi, Marcie Jammeh, Daba Marena, Ebou Lowe, Alpha Bah, Malafi Corr, the April 10 student protesters, attempting to kill Lawyer Ousman Sillah, the list goes on and on, what will stop him from denying killing the death row inmates?

There is an overwhelming evidence linking Jammeh to the killing of the folks mentioned above. His own assassin team confessed to us for having been assigned by Jammeh to kill the named folks. Jammeh is a liar, who should not be trusted. Senegal should be cautious. Please double check your facts if you have any.

Macky Sall and his team should watch the GRTS tape on Koriteh day, in which Jammeh swore to the Holly Quran that he will kill the death row inmates. We heard Jammeh bluntly telling the Muslim elders while swearing: "Belai Wali Talaiyi, if I don't kill the death row inmates, I will drink alcohol and eat pork."

A sober minded President who worth his salt will not speak like Jammeh. His statement was kind of an embarrassment to Gambians because it exposes his immaturity, and lack of Presidential qualities.

What the idiotic Gambian President fails to realize is that: each time he opens his dirty mouth, he represents the entire country. He is not representing one religious faith. The Gambia is a secular state. He should respect all faiths.

There were Muslim and Christian religious leaders present at the meeting. His stupid talk about him drinking alcohol and eating pork could be viewed as an attack against Christians. What does executing a supposed constitutional mandate has to do with drinking alcohol and eating pork? Jammeh has gone nuts for real folks.

No one is saying that the constitution do not prescribe for the execution of condemned prisoners. But the method of its application is our beef we the sane Gambians, Americans, British, and other nationals. The method of its application was dead wrong!

Hiding under the cover of darkness to kidnap and kill inmates—some of whom had appeal cases pending in the courts is an obstruction of Justice. Lamin Darboe, one of the executed inmates, had an appeal before the Supreme Court. He has been fighting very hard in the courts to have his death sentence dismissed. I spoke to Lamin Darboe while he was in prison months before his murder by the Kanilai monster. Lamin informed me that he needed financial help to finance his pending appeal. He said money was his problem, and he solicited my help. At the time, I was investigating a story relating to a prison riot, in which some inmates embarked on a hunger strike. Mr. Darboe confirmed the hunger strike and demanded the intervention of Red Cross and other human right groups to come to their aid.

I was also able to speak with Tamsir Jasseh, the former Immigration Director, who was sentenced to twenty years in prison on his alleged role in the March 2006 abortive coup. Mr. Jasseh was concerned about the plight of inmates at Mile Two. He asked me if I could highlight their plight on my newspaper so that an amnesty could be granted to the prisoners with good conduct.

Barely less than one year down the road, Mr. Jasseh was released from prison custody together with Dr. Amadou Scattered Janneh, who was sentenced to life imprisonment for merely distributing anti Government t shirts—calling for the end of dictatorship in the Gambia. Rev. Jesse Jackson Sr. secured their release amid intense negotiations with the Gambian leader to free the naturalized Gambian American nationals.

Mr. Jackson returned to the United States with the two prisoners. His successful Banjul trip was widely reported by America's mainstream media. The Gambian dictator paid for Jackson's trip expenses including that of Tamsir Jasseh and Dr. Amadou Scattered Janneh. The US State Department was never involved in the negotiations for the release of the American prisoners in the Gambia. It was a private initiative spearheaded by Rev. Jackson. This followed an invitation extended to Mr. Jackson by the Gambian President to visit him after he (Jammeh) agreed to halt the execution of the death row inmates.

"**The government** of the Gambia hereby informs the general public that contrary to the widespread rumors and speculations on the pronouncement made by his Excellency the president of the Republic on the implementation of the death penalty in the Gambia; it wishes to state for the records that such irresponsible spreading of information is wrong," The government press release stated. (Question: What rumor is being spread in town? What wrong is the regime talking about that needed to be corrected? Who are the folks rumoring about Jammeh's implementation of the death penalty in the Gambia? The introduction of the government press release is not only ambiguous, but vague in its entirety. It puzzles the reader's mind on the first reading of the poorly written press release. Instead of denying or confirming the veracity of the executions as reported by the International media, Jammeh and his cronies embarked on blame game as usual. What the regime has done essentially is: casting aspersion in the minds of Gambians. The press release does not address the issues. It instead compounded the rumors they lamented about. One would have expected any responsible government to come up a better story, or lies if you may call it; than

46

further confusing the situation. The regime never denied that the nine prisoners have not been killed. It also never justified the killings in the rambling press release.)

"**The laws of the Gambia** on death penalty are very clear and provides under Section 18(1) of the constitution of the Republic of the Gambia states that no Person shall be deprived of his or her lives intentionally; except in the execution of a sentence of death imposed by a court of competent jurisdiction in respect of criminal offence for which the penalty is death under the laws of the Gambia as they have effects in accordance with subsection 2 of which he or she has lawfully been convicted in due compliance with the provisions of the law as above." (Comments: Yes, the said constitutional provision do exists, but the same constitution that you invoked also advocates for the observance of the due process of the law. In this case, there was no due process observed. Inmates who had pending appeal cases before the courts were executed. Let the regime furnish us with court papers showing that all the executed inmates had exhausted their appeals, or trials before the Friday gruesome incident. We need the proofs in order to be convinced. We also read somewhere that before such killings can be carried out the National Assembly must be put in the picture. In this case, there was notification brought before the floor of the National Assembly. The Kanilai monster acted alone in carrying out the secret executions).

"**It follows that** all persons on death row have been tried by the Gambian courts of competent jurisdiction and thereof convicted and sentence to death in accordance with the law. They have exhausted all their legal rights of appeal as provided by the law." (Comments: Again, you are trying to justify the secret executions. The legal process being exhausted does not give you the right to hide under the cover of darkness to kill inmates. The Gambia is supposedly a country of laws, why don't you invite independent observers, and other branches of the Government to witness your callous actions? Is it because Jammeh had sworn to kill these people that's why the killings were expedited without conforming to the dictates of the constitution? Oh my God, Gambians are in deep trouble! One man is deciding the fate of about two million people. He kills our people without following the dictates of the constitution. In my view, there is no constitution in the Gambia. It's Jammeh's constitution).

"The general public is hereby warned that the peace and stability of our beloved nation as regards to protection of the lives, liberty and property of individuals must at all cost be preserved and jealously guarded." (Comments: Why talking about the protection of lives, liberty and property of Gambians, when you have undermined that very provision of the constitution. Why don't you avail the inmates the right to explore the due process of the law? Why killing these people overnight? If your statement is to go by: Why is the President running an alleged secret assassin team in the Gambia? Who authorizes Mr. Jammeh to kill our people as he desires? We will live you with the above questions until history catches up with the dictatorship. You will have your day in court).

The entire nation has been stunned by dictator Yaya Jammeh's last minute confession of secretly killing the death row inmates. Yes, the mentally impaired De Facto Gambian leader has admitted that he has indeed killed the "mile two nine," as it is called in town, without following the dictates of the constitution. Mr. Jammeh unilaterally acted alone without consulting with his cabinet to kill the inmates. There was no legal paperwork obtained that could justify the killings. Jammeh merely picked up the phone and ordered for their execution and it was done without delay under the cover of darkness. Impunity is at its best in the Gambia.

Jammeh often brags that Friday is his day. And he is damn right. He perpetrates most of his alleged secret killings on a Thursday night, and the following morning on a Friday, the nation would be left second guessing as to who must have perpetrated such mysterious killings. Jammeh allegedly killed Deyda Hydara on a Thursday night, and he repeated the same trend in the case of the mile two nine inmates.

Jammeh's admission of killing the nine inmates will no doubt have far reaching political ramifications for our country. For example, if he is allowed to go scot free, he will continue to target political opponents, journalists, public servants, and members of the security forces.

Mr. Jammeh is testing the reaction of Gambians, including the international community. He should not be allowed to get away with his alleged crimes. It is time for action Gambia. Let us take our country back from this monster. If it means demonstrating until his regime falls it worth it.

Analyzing The Regime's Press Release

PRESS RELEASE

WARRANT/ORDER FOR EXECUTION

Please find attached a Press Release on the above subject matter. I shall be grateful if you could announce the attached Press Release on the Radio and Television in English and the local languages with immediate effect.

Assan Tangara

FOR: PERMANENT SECRETARY

Tel: (002220) 4228710!4228611

Fax (002220)420132014223877

Following the convictions and pronouncements of death sentences by the Gambian Courts of competent jurisdiction and further to the exhaustion of their appeals, the Ministry of Interior wishes to inform the general public that the following convicts were executed by firing squad on Sunday 26th August, 2012: Comments: Here you lied again. Where was the executions carried out? Who witnessed the secret executions? This regime is foolish and full of it. You think that you are talking to laymen. By the way, what does the constitution says about the enforcement of the death penalty? Did you truly conform to the dictates of the constitution? You know for a fact that the killings were carried out illegally. One man called Yaya Jammeh just wake up one morning and decreed that these people should be killed. His Justice Minister Lamin Jobarteh dares say that he was consulted. The national Assembly was also not contacted. Jammeh's own cabinet, including Isatou Njie Saidy were never put in the picture beside what they witnessed on Koriteh day at the State House, where Jammeh vowed to execute the death row inmates. Jammeh's actions tantamount to genocide. He also allegedly lied that these people were killed by a firing squad. That's a fat lie. The inmates were executed through lethal injection. Jammeh's inside job secret killings came to light when the Freedom Newspaper broke the story on Friday morning. Amnesty international corroborated our piece by quoting credible sources to support our story. At first, Jammeh wanted to keep Gambians and the world out of the loop. He even allegedly lied to the visiting African Union envoy by telling him that he never meant to kill the inmates—that he just wanted to scare would-be criminals. Jammeh made similar lies to his next door neighbor Senegalese President Macky Sall. He told Macky that no one was killed. When the pressure intensified on him to welcome human rights groups, families, and foreign diplomats accredited to the Gambia to visit the mile two prison to see the prisoners, Jammeh budged. That was the time he came up with the lie that the nine inmates were executed on Sunday, knowing very well that the killings were carried out on Thursday night. Jammeh is a pathological liar. No one should take him seriously.

1. **DAWDA BOJANG**

Charged with offence of the brutal and gruesome murder of RONALD STANLEY FORD a British National contrary to section 187 of the Criminal Code Cap. 10 Vol III of the Laws of The Gambia 1990. He was convicted by the Kanifing Magistrates Court on 29 August 2007 and sentenced to life. He appealed the life sentence which was dismissed and substituted to death, pursuant to Section 188 of the Criminal Code Cap. 10, Vol. Ill of the Laws of the Gambia 1990 on 30th July, 2010. (Comments: What court dismissed his appeal? Why don't you accompany court papers with the press release to at least to support your lies? Was Dawda Bojang's family informed about his execution? There was no notification send out to the families about Jammeh's unilateral decision to take the lives of the inmates. The fact of the matter is that there is no law in the Gambia. Jammeh uses the courts and the security forces as his power base to perpetrate criminality against our oppressed people. The same Yaya Jammeh told us on Koriteh day that he will drink alcohol and eat pork if he doesn't fulfill his promise to execute the inmates. And he has indeed fulfilled his promise. The mile two nine are gone. He has killed them. No decent burial was accorded to them. Who knows if Jammeh uses their remains to feed his animals in Kanilai (I mean the crocodiles)? He is broke).

2. MALANG SONKO

Charged with the offence of the murder of one *BUBA JAWAR4* by hitting him with a wooden stick on his neck thereby causing his death. Contrary to Section 187 of the Criminal Code Cap. 10, Vol. III Laws of The Gambia. He was convicted by the Brikama Magistrates Court and sentenced to Death on January 30th1 2012. No appeal was filed by the convict.

3. EX LIEUTENANT LAMIN JARJOU

4. EX SGT. alias Ex Lt. ALIEU BAH

5. EX SGT. LAMIN F. JAMMEH

The trio were charged with two counts of treason, two counts of murder of LANCE CORPORAL KEBBA DRAMMEH and PRIVATE BAKARY CEESAY, 4 counts of unlawful wounding with intent to do grievous harm, two counts of Robbery and two counts of abduction contrary to section 35, 187, 212, 273 and 236 respectively of the Criminal Code, Cap. 10, Vol. III of the Laws of The Gambia 1990. They were convicted and sentenced to death by the High Court of The Gambia with three Judges sitting on the 27th of October, 1998. Their appeals were dismissed and there were no further appeal. (Comments: Granted, their appeals were dismissed, but why don't you notify their families about the planned executions? Don't you think that they deserve to bid farewell to their families before being executed? The entire process surrounding the execution of the inmates was a sham. The regime acted extra judicially without following the dictates of the constitution. There was no death certificate presented to the affected families. Besides, what we have been told that the President signed for their death warrant).

6. **TABARA SAMBA**

Charged with the offence of the murder of EBRIMA NYANG her husband on account of marrying a second wife poured hot cooking oil on him at Jeshwang thereby causing his death, contrary to Section 187 of the Criminal Code Cap. 10, Vol. III of the Laws of The Gambia 1990. She was convicted on the 26th of September, 2007 and sentenced to death. She appealed to the High Court of The Gambia, which appeal was dismissed. (Comments: No one is saying that the constitution did not mandate Jammeh to enforce the death penalty. Our beef is: the method of its application. We mean the way Jammeh is going about enforcing the death penalty is wrong. Anything done, or executed under the cover of darkness is illegal. The Gambia is supposedly a country of laws, and we expect the sick Gambian dictator to conform to the laws of the land. He is not above the law. He doesn't own the Gambia and her people. Ms. Tabara Samba's family ought to have been informed about her execution. The Senegalese Government too should have been informed as well about the killings ahead of time. The families of the former army officers said they were never informed about the execution. They read the news like any other Gambian on the papers. The Senegalese government was never notified about the killing of their nationals. Jammeh killed Tabara Samba without informing Senegal and her family. President Macky Sall is being tested by Jammeh. It all depends on how he reacts to the killing of two of his nationals by the Kanilai monster without legal sanctioning. The bogus press release is nothing, but a damage control. One could read a sign of guilt on the side of Jammeh for having perpetrated such a heinous crime and now he has been busted. Jammeh never thought that the secret killings would have been uncovered by the Freedom Newspaper. We are the first media outlet to break the story—thanks to our dependable sources on the ground. This is the medium policing Jammeh round the clock. Without the Freedom Newspaper, some of his alleged crimes against humanity would have been buried under the carpet. That's why the media needs to be supported and encouraged to expose power excesses and human rights abuses allegedly carried out by reckless leaders like Jammeh. There should be an independent media that should relate the Gambian story. The Freedom Newspaper is now part and parcel of Jammeh's one man Government agenda. He always thinks about what would be the Freedom Newspaper's reaction on his pronouncements and policies. That's a good thing for the country. Now there is a formidable force keeping Jammeh honest).

7. **BUBA YARBOE**

Charged for the gruesome and brutal murder of her biological mother JAINABA JARJOU at Busumbala by hitting her on the head with an iron rod thereby causing her death Contrary to Sectión 187 of the Criminal Code, Cap lO, Vol. III Laws of The Gambia, 1990. He was convicted and sentenced to death by the High Court on November 3, 2010. He did not appeal against his sentence and conviction. (Comments: At least you are being truthful in the case of Buba Yarboe. That, Jammeh executed him without availing him with the legal opportunity to file an appeal. This is the height of injustice. A travesty of justice for that matter. How dare that you executed a man who never contested his death sentence? Do you bother to find out if he is faced with financial constraints to file an appeal before the courts? The financial cost involved in criminal litigation in the Gambia is exorbitant. There are very few death row inmates in the Gambia who can afford to pay a lawyer for representation. The government legal aid accorded to inmates is not sufficient. Most of the lawyers reluctantly accept cases. They will tell you that it is not worth taking because there is no money at the end of the day. In addition to that, the courts are infested with Nigerian mercenary judges. Inmates are not assured of justice since the President dictates what goes around the judiciary. Judges who do not toe Jammeh's line are yanked out of the judiciary. That is what you call justice Gambia? A Gambia, in which the President can overrule the courts. He kills inmates without legal sanctioning. He sacks judges as he pleases).

8. **LAMIN B S DARBOE**

He was charged with the offence of the brutal murder of MUHAMMED OULD FAAL, a Mauritanian National, by hitting him with a blunt object on the head on the 2nd April 1985 at Sinchu Alagie in the Kombo North, contrary to Section 187 of the Criminal Code Cap.. 10 Vol. III of the Laws of The Gambia 1990. Pursuant to Section 188 of the Criminal Code Cap. 10, Vol. III, he was convicted and sentenced to death on the 3rd December, 1986. He appealed against conviction and sentenced on 13th day of June 1988 and the said appeal was dismissed. (Comments: Here you are lying again! Lamin Darboe had a pending appeal before the Supreme Court. I was made to understand that he engaged the services of a Gambian lawyer to help him fight his freedom in court. I could not independently verify this info with the lawyer, but a source texted me the very day we reported Lamin's execution informing me that Lamin Darboe was sentenced to 26 years in jail and his jail term was supposed to be completed in 2012. Jammeh allegedly uses his position to revoke his sentence, following a prison riots at the mile two prisons and he was condemned to death. There was no legal pronouncement sentencing Lamin Darboe to death. Jammeh accused Mr. Darboe of taking part in a prison riots. At the time Baboucarr Jatta was the Minister of Interior. Lamin has always been a good prisoner, according to sources. He has always maintained a good conduct. "In fact, he recently filed an appeal in the courts to fight for his release. A friend of mine sent him some money for his court fee to pay his lawyer," a source told me in a text message. A man who served almost 26 years in prison has been killed by Jammeh. He could have been rehabilitated to serve as a role model in our prison system. But you tell that to a sane leader. Jammeh has gone nuts).

9. **GEBE BAH**

He was charged for the murder of one NJUGA SAMBA by causing him a deep stab wound on the left ear side of the head on the 18th December 1997 at Mariama Kunda village in the Kombo North District, Western Region. Judgment was delivered on the 30th day of January 2004 in which the accused was sentenced to death. He appealed the conviction which was dismissed. (Comments: Like Tabara Samba, Gebe Bah too was executed without the knowledge of his family and government back home in Senegal. Why the executions now? Is it because Jammeh is fulfilling the alleged rituals that was prescribed to him by a marabout? Jammeh allegedly believed that by spilling human blood it will save him from not losing power. What a wishful thinking. He treats inmates like Guinea pigs. He thinks that he can kill them without people knowing about it. This is sad Gambia. Senegal should not let Jammeh go scot free with his alleged crimes. He should be made accountable for his actions).

The General Public is hereby warned that the rule of law as regards the peace and stability and the protection of lives, property and liberty will not be compromised for whatever reason. That all acts of violence, criminal activities and indiscipline resulting to murder, treason, arson, trafficking in drugs and humans and the likes of such offences attracting death sentences shall not be tolerated. Therefore, all sentences as prescribed by law will be carried out to the letter including the death penalty. (Comments: The last sentence sounds like a threat to me. It implies that Jammeh is determined to carry out more executions in days to come if he is not stopped. You do not talk about the need for the respect of the rule of law and civil liberties, when the man entrusted with steering the affairs of the nations is behaving otherwise. It's Yaya Jammeh who is allegedly killing our people without legal sanctioning. It's Yaya Jammeh, who is stealing from our people. It is Yaya Jammeh, who is undermining the constitution day in day out. Stop talking about the need to safeguard law when the people running the country are holding its subjects onto ransom. The economic and political crimes allegedly committed by Jammeh since coming to power is unimaginable. It is just too much to illustrate in one write up).

The General Public is further called to respect the Fundamental Human Rights of All Citizens and Residents in the Republic of The Gambia. The Republic of The Gambia is a sovereign state which, like other sovereign states currently implementing the death penalty, has the right to implement its domestic laws as stipulated in her constitution. (Comments: The Gambia doesn't fall under the category of democratic nations. The death penalty is applied in countries where the rule of law is respected. The courts are independent in those countries, unlike the Gambia, in which the mafia can use their influence to dictate judicial proceedings. The false pretense should stop on the side of Jammeh and his team. There is no semblance of justice in the Gambia. The sovereignty you talking about is a lie. A sovereign nation will not heavily rely on rogue judges, lawyers, and magistrates from Nigeria to decide the fate of its people. Our courts are manned by non Gambians. Sadly, the President of Gambia's Appeal Court Joseph Wowo used to be an undocumented illegal alien in the United States. This is the guy entrusted to oversee our justice system. He left the US due to out of frustration, and desperation. Now he is on Jammeh's mafia judicial payroll. Gambians should rise up and take their country back. There is no government in the Gambia. What we have; is a bunch of inexperienced folks running around town claiming to be representing a nation. If you fail to act, more innocent folks will die in the hands of this heartless despot).

CHAPTER FIVE

THE AFTERMATH OF THE EXECUTION OF THE DEATH ROW INMATES

Gambian journalist Abubacarr Saidykhan, and his colleague Baboucarr Ceeesay, left their homes to respond to an invitation extended to them by one senior police officer Musa Ndong, who tricked them with a misleading news that their application for permit to hold a peaceful demonstration against the death penalty has been approved by the police command, only to find themselves in police cells after they were told minutes after their arrival at the police headquarters in Banjul that they were under arrest. One Mr. Kinteh, a police officer was among the officers who processed the detained journalists.

Legally, it's permissible to hold a peaceful demonstration in the Gambia, but Mr. Saidykhan said the police told them that their application for permit tantamount to the breach of the law. However, Mr. Saidykhan strongly disagrees. He said they were exercising their right under the constitution to hold a peaceful protest. The journalists even asked for police escort.

The state in response, slammed Mr. Saidykan and his colleague with a felonious charge, which attracts seven years imprisonment with hard labor, without an option of a court fine, if found guilty. They were previously charged with conspiring to incite violence, but the police decided to drop the charge, and indicted them for attempting to commit felony.

Mr. Saidykhan remains hopeful about the outcome of his case. He says he is convinced that with a fair trial, he is confident of securing his freedom back. He is currently placed on bail pending the conclusion of the case.

Both Mr. Saidykan, and Ceesay were bit apprehensive about officer Ndong's invitation—given the short timeline for their permit application, and its subsequent approval on the same day, but the journalists wasted no time in showing up at the police headquarters.

Mr. Ndong works at the police Registry. He informed Saidykhan and Ceesay that the Inspector General of police Yankuba Sonko was supposed to process their application for permit to organize a peaceful protest, but Sonko at the material time was at the police training school conducting other official business.

The detained journalists were separated from each other throughout their detention. They were moved from one police station to the other, while detectives subjected them to rigorous and grilling interviews about the main motive behind their permit application.

Mr. Saidykhan said police did not buy their story that it was only two of them who were behind the planned protest march. Saidykhan said the police thought that there was an outside influence for the demonstration that was scheduled to take place on a Friday, if all plans worked out well.

But the journalists maintained throughout their police interviews that there was no outside influence for their planned demonstration and that they acted in line with the dictates of law by filing for permit application.

Mr. Saidykhan said both him and his colleague Baboucarr Ceesay are fully aware of the various provisions of the Criminal Procedure Code, which gave Gambians the right to organize a peaceful march upon obtaining a police permit. He said the detectives also wanted them to disclose whether the planned demonstration was prearranged, or discussed with any group of Gambians before applying for permit.

Saidykhan said he told the police that "mobilizing people for demonstration before applying for police permit could tantamount to undermining the laws of the Gambia." He said they are peaceful and law abiding Gambians who applied for permit in accordance with the dictates of the laws of the Gambia.

He says they never conspired to break the laws of the Gambia. All our actions were well intended and done in the best interest of the country, and her people, Mr. Saidykhan told Freedom Newspaper.

Police told Saidykhan and his co accused person that the main reason for their permit application was to protest against the execution of the nine death row inmates. Police also grilled the journalists to explain why they had to wait until the inmates were executed and applied for permit. The journalists in response said their application for permit was done in good faith as good citizens of the Gambia.

Mr. Saidykhan said the police also wanted to access their email addresses to see if the planned demonstration was discussed with other folks. Both Saidykhan and Ceesay declined the police request—arguing that such an action could be interpreted as intruding into their privacies.

That did not stop their interrogators from making further request to look into their social media activities. Police also wanted to search into their Facebook accounts to see who they befriended on their profile list. The journalists again maintained that they cannot allow anyone to access their Facebook accounts. Police conducted some random search on the web without accessing their Facebook accounts to see who they were talking to on Facebook before applying for a permit.

After their failed attempts to access the journalists email accounts, Mr. Saidykhan said he was confronted with questions about his past affiliation with the US based Freedom Newspaper. Mr. Saidykhan briefly served as a Freedom Newspaper Banjul Correspondent. He said the police downloaded in his presence the past stories he filed to the Freedom Newspaper bearing his byline. He says the police OC present during the investigations informed him that he doesn't see anything subversive in some of the stories he filed with the Freedom Newspaper.

According to Mr. Saidykhan, he told the police that his affiliation with the Freedom Newspaper was no secret to Gambians. His published commentaries were accompanied with his picture, and byline. He said he was not doing anything illegal by filing news reports to the Freedom Newspaper.

For journalist Baboucarr Ceesay, Saidykhan said the police confronted him with questions about his affiliation with the African Review online newspaper. He said the police wanted to know how Ceesay was contracted to report for the foreign media among other things. Ceesay in turn furnished them with the necessary information they sought for, he said.

After exhaustive police interviews, Mr. Saidykhan said the police then asked him to accompany them at his home to search his room for possible subversive materials. Saidykhan lives in Eboe Town, just in the suburb of a Commercial City called Serre-Kunda. At this time, police had already obtained information about his educational background, place of residence, date of birth, biological parents and so on. The journalists were confined into different single man cells throughout their detention.

Police made three trips to Saidykhan's home. On the first trip, the officers said they do not believe that Saidykhan had taken them to his actual room. They searched the room and left. They thought that the journalist tried to deceive them by taking them to a wrong room.

On their second trip, Saidykhan said the police requested to enter his brother's room Ousman Saidykhan, who was not at home at the time. Police searched his parent's room before proceeding to his other sibling's room. Police left without finding any incriminating materials against Mr. Saidykhan.

On their third trip to the house, police forcefully broke into Abubacarr Saidykhan's brother's room. The officers numbering six asked for

Ousman Saidykhan, and they were told that he was in Banjul to locate his detained brother. The officers then contracted a welder man in the neighborhood to dismantle Ousman Saidykhan's window, where they jumped into the room to conduct a search, Saidykhan said.

Mr. Saidykhan said he was not aware of any search warrant obtain by the police to break into his brother's room to conduct a search. "I was informed about their intention to search my brother's room inside the car, while being escorted to my home. There was no search warrant sought to break the window—not to mention conducting a search. The window was completely vandalized. I watched the welder man breaking the window in my presence. I know him. He is my neighbor," Mr. Saidykha said.

After breaking into his brother's room, Saidykhan said the police left with him without any subversive evidence found in the room. He was placed back in his cell, where he stayed until his release.

Mr. Saidykhan and Ceesay spent four days in police custody before they were granted bail. The constitution says the police should not detain people for more than 72 hours, but according to Saidykhan the police exceeded the timeline stipulated by the constitution in regards to the detention of accused suspects. The state later dropped charges it filed against Saidykhan and Ceesay.

After devastating the world with his well fulfilled promise of executing the death row inmates, Gambia's delusional, and psychopathic leader Yahya Jammeh has now turned his attention to the private media. This past weekend witnessed the closure of two newspapers in the Gambia after its publishers were ordered to cease publication with immediate effect. The President's office has decreed that the Standard Newspaper and the Daily News Newspaper should be yanked out of the news stand—although no reason was given for the directive. The Editors were left to either comply with the Presidential order, or risked facing the consequences.

The Standard Newspaper is owned by Sheriff Bojang, a prolific Gambian writer, and also a onetime Managing Director of the

Pro-government Newspaper, the Daily Observer, while Madi Ceesay, former Press Union President, is the proprietor of the critical Daily News Newspaper. The press owners have confirmed to journalists that they were indeed ordered by the State House to cease publication.

The order came around the expiration of the deadline given by dictator Jammeh, who vowed that by mid September he will be done with the execution of all death row inmates in the Gambia. Although Mr. Jammeh has taken a shift on his promise amid international pressure to spare the lives of the remaining inmates.

The dictator has declared that he will halt the executions. He accepted an appeal made by the visiting Senegalese former Prime Minister Sulayman Ndeneh Njie to halt the killings.

Administration sources said Jammeh is unhappy with the Standard and the Daily News newspapers due to the Editors failure to write favorable editorials defending his execution of the death row inmates. The President was expecting a home based media coverage to legitimize his unilateral decision to take the lives of the inmates in the face of global condemnation.

The Daily Observer, a paper owned by Jammeh did a pretty good job in defending Jammeh, including his cabinet, some unprincipled religious leaders, and so called Council of elders.

The likes of Isatou Njie Saidy, Justice Minister Jobarteh, Lamin Waa Juwara, Ousman Sonko, and Njogu Bah emerged as Jammeh's image maker during the national mayhem. They were tasked to clean up Jammeh's mess. The folks mentioned herein openly misled the nation in defense of Jammeh's alleged crimes against our people and country.

The Standard and the Daily News ensured that there was some degree of fair coverage during Jammeh's latest genocide against the Gambia and her people by seeking the reaction of the opposition leaders and all parties interested in justice. This angered the Kanilai monster. He felt rejected by the private press. He wants the entire nation to be complicit in his crimes against humanity. But little did despot Jammeh realize that there are honest Gambians in this country. The media is not that gullible to be used to legitimize his crimes.

No wonder that his novice Mayor and propagandist Yankuba Colley deplored the silence of some Gambians during what he calls "in time of need." Colley said the executions will service as a lesson to the administration. That the folks they thought were in support of Jammeh went into silence during such a national crisis.

Yanks take note: Gambians are hard to predict. You will be shocked to learn that the folks claiming to be one hundred percent APRC will be the first to disown Jammeh if he was to be deposed today. There are few real Gambians in today's Gambia. The APRC and Jammeh are enjoying blinded support. I mean there are folks supporting your President against their own will. Gambians don't like Yahya Jammeh.

The true realists are some of us telling the Gambian story as it is. We care less about how Jammeh, or Yanks Colley feels about our political opinion. We cherish this country and her people. We will continue to fight and die for the Gambia. You get that Yanks! After all, this country is for all of us. It doesn't belong to Jammeh, or Yanks Colley. It's our Gambia!

Any media house that worth its salt should not ignore Jammeh's crimes. The executions were carried out illegally. That's why Jammeh's public support has dwindled. He has created more enemies today than ever before. Stop the propaganda and face the realities of the day the APRC.

A BBC Correspondent based in Dakar, Senegal was also expelled from the country. He secured a visa from the Gambian High Commission in Dakar, but only to be declared unwelcomed in the country, upon his landing at the Banjul International airport. The BBC Correspondent was assigned to cover the execution of the nine death row inmates in the Gambia. Despite the intervention of the British High Commission in Banjul for the Gambian authorities to reconsider their decision, the BBC Correspondent was asked to leave the country.

As Gambia's erratic leader Yahya Jammeh has made a solemn promise to the visiting Senegalese former Prime Minister Sulayman Ndeneh Njie that he will discontinue his globally condemned execution of the death row inmates, the veteran United States Civil Rights Activist Reverend Jesse L. Jackson Sr. is set to visit Banjul to meet with the mentally impaired Gambian leader to make a total halt on the executions. In a passionate letter channeled through Gambia's Foreign Minister Momodou Tangara, and was addressed to Jammeh, Mr. Jackson appealed to the Gambian dictator to cease the execution of the death row inmates.

Mr. Jackson is the founder of the Rainbow Push Coalition. "As a friend of your beloved country, the Gambia, I am very concern about the global reputation and standing of your country as a result of the execution of the nine prisoners few days ago. I strongly appeal to you as a human and civil rights activist to please halt the execution of the remaining death row inmates," Mr. Jackson pleaded with Jammeh.

Jackson says he is "aware of the charges, trial, and conviction of these prisoners and I am not defending the crimes they committed. My appeal to you is on humanitarian grounds, as I respect the sovereignty of your country. I would like to travel to the Gambia to meet with you and discuss this very vital and urgent issue as soon as possible. I look forward to hearing from you as soon as possible."

Mr. Jackson was also concerned about other regional issues facing the Gambia, such as poverty reduction, developmental challenges, security and peace. He offered prayers for the country and her people.

"I continue to pray for you and all Gambians as you face other national and regional issues such as fighting poverty, development, security, and peace. I pray for the families of those murdered by these prisoners and I hope that, as difficult as it may be, our faith will guide us through," said the Civil Rights Leader.

It is imperative to note that Mr. Jammeh has been increasingly isolated by the international community due to his flagrant rights abuses. He has been over the years lobbying to meet with influential American policymakers, and lobbyists in a bid to market his battered image.

Mr. Jackson proposing to meet with Jammeh means a lot to the Gambian despot. The Jackson Banjul trip will be another political showcase on the side of the Jammeh propaganda machine to fool the populace of the impoverished nation—that mighty America is pleading with him to spare the lives of the death row inmates.

Mr. Jammeh is an attention seeker. Mr. Jackson should be ready to meet with an irrational leader, full of controversies. Be forewarned that you are meeting with a leader, who is suffering from attention deficiency. Half of the time Jammeh will open his eyes, but hardly keeps up with the flow of any serious conversation. Take note of fact number one.

Fact number two: You will also learn about his communication shortcomings. Jammeh's communication skills shocked. You might need an interpreter to accompany you to the State House to comprehend him. He is not an intelligent communicator at all. One has to be very familiar with him be able to make sense out of some of his stupid remarks about sub-regional issues and post colonialism era. Do not be surprised if he starts lecturing you about slavery, the history of Kunta Kinteh, and Zionism.

Fact number three: Jammeh is a delusional leader, who claims to have bagged numerous doctorate degrees—though he has never acquired any university education. He is a buffoonery leader, who enjoyed to be in the limelight at all times. He also claims to have cure for aids, diabetes, asthma, infertility, high blood pressure, and other ailments. I am sure you are aware of his false claim for having cure for aids. This is just a heads up! Do not be taken by surprise if he takes you around his clinic in Kanilai.

Fact Number Four: Mr. Jackson another thing that you need to know about Jammeh is: his personal love for animals. If he doesn't take you to his zoo in Kanilai, please do ask him to take you to the zoo. You will be amazed by the number of endangered spices in that zoo.

Just for a word of advice Rev. Jackson: Do not get close to the lions! These are wild lions. Do not make the mistake to get close to the crocodile pond as well. There is also a fish pond where you can spend time with Jammeh to enjoy nature. Snakes, zebra, and other wild animals are all over the place.

Fact Number Five: Mind you: This is a country in which about eighty percent of the population is living in abject poverty. Yet its leader can afford to spend millions of dollars annually to feed his animals. You can feel the suffering of the Gambian masses once you tour around the city Banjul. It is evident on people's faces. Everyone is hopeless in that country.

Please use your Banjul trip to urge Jammeh to stop the wasteful spending and his flamboyance life style. You should also consider appealing to Jammeh to stop perpetrating, or condoning corruption in his regime. Eighteen years of Jammeh's rule has transformed this country as one of the poorest countries in the world. Mr. Jammeh cannot distinguish between what is state property and personal property. He allegedly steals from Gambians on a daily basis. You need to talk to him to stop stealing from Gambian taxpayers. He has bought a house for his Moroccan wife in the Potomac Maryland area. Jammeh's wife has also bought a house in Canada. She also owns businesses in France, Morocco, and Guinea Conakry. Her frequent shuttling between Banjul, Washington, France, Canada, and Morocco is costing Gambian taxpayers millions of United States dollars. Mr. Jammeh can afford to pay for his wife's unfinished overseas travels and yet our people are starving. The country's healthcare, economy, education sector, and infrastructure are on the verge of total collapse.

Fact Number Six: Jammeh should consider handing over the country. He has no clue as to how to run a country. Jammeh represents underdevelopment. He has retarded Gambia's development. His leadership brought economic hardship and miseries for Gambians.

Fact Number Seven: Jammeh may be entertaining Rev. Jackson, but his inner character is deceptive. He allegedly worships idols. He allegedly sacrifices human beings in the name of consolidating himself into power.

Fact Number Eight: Rev. Jackson your proposed Banjul trip is timely. Timely in the sense that it came at a time, when dictator Jammeh decided to close down two private newspapers in the Gambia: the Standard Newspaper and the Daily News Newspaper. All these happened; in the wake of his so called declaration to impose moratorium on the remaining death row inmates. A private FM Radio station called Teranga FM has also been shut down by the dictator.

We need your intervention to prevail on Africa's mad leader to reopen the said media houses in the interest of peace and democracy. Safe journey Rev. Jackson. We look forward to seeing you back home in the United States.

Rev. Jesse Jackson, Sr is in Banjul to meet with Gambia's alleged career murderer dictator Yahya Jammeh. On arrival in Banjul, Jackson and his delegation were accorded with a rousing welcome. On arrival at the Banjul International airport, the Civil Rights Leader took a photograph with Jammeh's co partners in crime notably: our alleged mercenary Justice Minister Lamin Jobarteh, and the disgraceful SG Njogu Bah. Jackson met with the most despicable characters in Jammeh's regime. Jobarteh and Njogu Bah have been transformed as alleged assassins by the Kanilai monster. They are now part and parcel of the Jammeh alleged murder machine. The duo, openly defended the execution of the death row inmates, and even had the guts to lie to Gambians that Jammeh acted in line with the dictates of the constitution to execute the inmates.

Rev. Jesse Jackson, Sr clearly told the Fox News cable network that dictator Jammeh personally solicited him to pay him a visit after weeks of talking to the Gambian moron President on the phone. Jammeh's agenda is to use Jackson's trip as a public relations coup—in a bid to market his battered image locally and internationally. Bad timing fools! Jackson cannot clean your mess! Jammeh is an isolated President dying for relevance.

Mr. Jackson will not leave Banjul without his mission accomplish that we know. He has key demands for the Gambian tyrant: One, for Jammeh to commute the sentences of the remaining death row inmates. Two, for Jammeh to consider abolishing the death penalty if possible. Thirdly, for Jammeh to work toward restoring, or winning public confidence into his discredited regime.

Gambians should not be surprised if Jammeh announces to pardon some of the inmates in Mile Two serving life imprisonment. Dr. Amadou Scattered Janneh, Tamsir Jasseh, both American subjects come to mind on Jackson peace trip. Mr. Jackson is likely to raise their plight with Jammeh.

It's unfortunate that Jammeh is politicizing the execution of the Mile Two Nine inmates. After illegally taking their lives, Jammeh is now banking on Jesse Jackson to help him market his image.

Mr. Jammeh should understand that the innocent lives that he has wasted in the name of fighting crimes in the Gambia cannot go unpunished. Jesse Jackson coming to the Gambia as a "special guest" of Jammeh will not mitigate the dictator's future prosecution for crimes against humanity. You allegedly killed these people on your own accord and therefore you must pay for the price one day.

Dictator Jammeh has that urge for self importance, egoistic tendencies, and personal glorification, when he is nothing but an imbecile. Mr. Jackson should not have wasted his precious time and energy meeting with such a fool! You reason with a human being and not a villain like Jammeh.

But on the other hand, it is imperative to note that Rev. Jesse Jackson has carried out important humanitarian missions on behalf of America dating back the era of former American President Bill Clinton. Mr. Jackson has helped to facilitate the release of Americans detained overseas time and time. Jackson is an American goodwill Ambassador. He wipes the tears of the suffering masses around the globe in times of need.

Therefore, his Banjul trip should be viewed as another humanitarian mission being spearheaded by an African American brother for that matter, who is trying to save the lives of an entire nation from a mentally impaired despot. Mr. Jackson is essentially trying to bring sense to Gambia's sick President to halt the killings, and work towards the empowerment and preservation of mankind and not otherwise. What a noble course!

In as much as Jammeh is mentally challenged, he should not let down Mr. Jackson. In other words, he should refrain from lying to Jackson just for the sake of trying to impress him. He should not promise what he cannot deliver. Be truthful and be yourself Mr. Jammeh.

The death penalty is never a solution in combating crimes. What the Gambia needs is: a sincere, honest, responsible and accountable government. One cannot talk about an impartial judicial system in the face of a polluted legal system dominated by Nigerian mercenary judges. One cannot talk about a just judiciary, when the very system that should enhance its efficiency is corrupt and weak to the core. One cannot talk about a fair trial, when the President is meddling into the affairs of the judiciary day in day out. The President allegedly dictates to judges about the outcome of pending cases. He occasionally allegedly recommends prison terms to be meted out to guilty accused persons. He recruits and sack judges at his own accord.

Mr. Jackson's concern about the possibilities of wrongly jailed inmates being executed is very legitimate. It is a legitimate concern. None of the executed inmates were accorded with a fair trial.

Based on credible information reaching us, some of the executed inmates had pending appeals in the courts. Jammeh ended the lives of the inmates without respecting the common legal saying: "innocent until proven guilty." The inmates have not entirely exhausted their appeal processes as dictated by the constitution. One cannot talk about or depend on the constitution in the Gambia, since Jammeh is the primary owner. He uses and abuses the constitution on his own accord.

We hope and pray that Jesse Jackson's trip will bear some fruits so that Gambians can finally be at peace for now. The Kanilai monster has been killing our people since he steps his foot at the State House.

He is now using the rogue courts to legitimize his alleged crimes, but us Gambians have been living with Jammeh's executions for eighteen solid years. Perhaps, the world is now getting a hint about Jammeh's underreported alleged crimes. This is the life we have been living all these years Mr. Jackson. Welcome to Jammeh's murder land.

On Monday September 17th 2012, Rev Jesse Jackson Sr secured the release of two American nationals held in Gambian jails on treason charges. Dr. Amadou Scattered Janneh and Tamsir Jasseh have been set free, and they are on their way back to the United States. The American Civil Rights Activist facilitated their release.

Janneh was jailed for life imprisonment after he was accused of printing a t-shirt calling for an end to dictatorship. For Tamsir Jasseh, a former police chief was jailed on coup related charges dating back in March of 2006. Jasseh is a retired United States soldier. He took part in the US Operations Desert Storm.

President Jammeh has agreed to free the inmates, but he insisted that both Janneh and Jasseh should leave the country. Jackson will accompany the inmates to the US on Tuesday.

In an editorial on Monday, the Freedom Newspaper Editor Pa Nderry M'Bai maintained that Mr. Jackson will not leave Banjul without his mission accomplished. Mr. M'Bai noted that Mr. Jackson has key demands for the Gambian tyrant: One, for Jammeh to commute the sentences of the remaining death row inmates. Two, for Jammeh to consider abolishing the death penalty if possible. Thirdly, for Jammeh to work toward restoring, or winning public confidence into his discredited regime.

Mr. M'Bai also predicted that Jackson will secure the release of Dr. Janneh and Tamsir Jasseh. And his prediction has been confirmed by the news of the release of the inmates. Dr. Amadou Scattered Janneh and Tamsir Jasseh have been released from state custody.

Rev. Jesse Jackson's Banjul trip has made dictator Yahya Jammeh a born again man—with the dictator learning how to forgive folks, who allegedly wronged him in the past—notably the jailed former public officials. Mr. Jammeh has begun opening the prison gates to free inmates convicted of economic crimes and other related crimes in the name of extending an amnesty to the convicts. There are big things happening in Banjul right now! Jackson's trip led to the opening of the prison gates. His host Mr. Jammeh is determined to clear the prisons. Former Secretary General and Head of the Civil Service Ousman Jammeh has been pardoned by the President, according to a news release from the State House. Also released on Tuesday was one Karafa Sanneh, the former Kanilai farm manager. The President said he has forgiven the inmates. Both Ousman Jammeh and Karafa Sanneh have reunited with their families.

The Gambian President is beginning to realize that the Gambia needs more productive citizens and not an overcrowded prison with inmates engaging into no creative ventures. Good start Jammeh! Let us clear the prisons.

Tamsir Jasseh and Amadou Janneh are now back in the US. The duo had their own stories to tell to the world about prison life. They couldn't believe when Jesse Jackson showed up and asked them to come follow him to go back where they called home the United States of America.

I personally spoke to Tamsir Jasseh, while he was in Mile Two as an inmate, matter of fact during a prison riots last year. The inmates were on a hunger strike. Tamsir was wondering if the Freedom Newspaper could highlight their plight to the world so that the US State Department, the Red Cross, Amnesty International and other right groups could come to their aid. And we did! Our coverage on the mile two inmates hunger strike warranted a taskforce from the Ministry of interior to visit the prison. Inmates were threatened with dire consequences if they continue with the strike.

I can vividly remember the Interior Minister Ousman Sonko denying any hunger strike at the Mile Two Prison. Now that Tamsir Jasseh has been released he can help to shed more light on the story.

We do not make up stories. Our stories are well sourced and grounded. This is to show to Jammeh how connected we are to the Gambia. We had access to so many establishments within and outside the government.

Jammeh has finally heeded to Jackson's advice to learn to be more compassionate, forgiving, and unifying as the leader of the Gambia. Jackson's trip has opened a new political chapter, and dispensation for the Gambia and her people.

We hope Mr. Jammeh will continue with his policy reforms and let go prisoners with good conduct for heaven sake. There are so many brains wasting at mile two, who could have been beneficial to the country. Prisons are meant to serve as correctional facilities, but in the case of the Gambia, prisons do not help to shape the lives of inmates. Instead, it makes them worst upon release from custody. There is absolute need to revamp our prison system so that folks graduating from the prison after serving their time will come home to become more productive citizens.

Mr. Jammeh will stand to gain a lot if he considers freeing the other coup inmates. He doesn't need to multiply his enemies list. As a wise counseling, he should also consider stepping down after his current mandate and concentrate on his farming. In that way, he will win the respect of the world and his critics. Power corrupt; absolute power corrupt. The more he stays in office, the likely he will outlive his productivity as a leader. We need a term limit for the presidency in the Gambia.

We welcomed President Jammeh's move to extend amnesty to the inmates. Dictatorship is not the future for Africa. It is not the way forward. Africa needs caring leaders, who are sensitive to the plight of its people. As the saying goes: "Be nice to others on your way up, so that when you are down, people can sympathize with you."

Jammeh should continue to extend similar amnesty to other inmates. He has nothing to lose by freeing inmates with good conduct in prison. Mam Sait Njie, Lie Joof, Lang Tombong Tamba, Ngorr Secka,

Momodou Gaye, and all the other inmates falsely jailed by the Nigerian mercenary judges should be freed.

Mr. Jammeh can start the reconciliation process now before his departure to save this country from a potential civil war. There are so many angry people nursing their pains quietly at their homes in the Gambia. Let us save this country from war.

A Pakistani security guard entrusted with securing the Gambian High Commission in London, had no alternative, but to let in the raging Gambian demonstrators into the Gambian Mission on Tuesday, after demonstrators insisted that they must walk into the High Commission to register their anger against the recent genocide allegedly carried out by Gambia's erratic leader dictator Yahya Jammeh, who murdered nine death row inmates in cold blood without conforming to the dictates of the country's constitution. The High Commission was completely deserted when the demonstrators walked into the premises. The High Commissioner and his staff abandoned the High Commission for their own personal safety.

The London showdown signals the end of Jammeh's regime. The demonstrators drank tea inside the High Commission, while the widely feared Gambian dictator's portraits were vandalized by the protesters.

The protesters occupied the High Commission for hours. They claimed that they have deposed dictator Jammeh from power. The protesters also freely walk around the offices of the High Commission. They chanted anti Jammeh slogans, while demanding for justice, human rights, good governance and free press in the Gambia.

There were files containing passport applications, and other relevant documents abandoned in the ghost High Commission office. The High Commissioner was nowhere to be seen. The staff deserted the premises.

One of the Protesters Siaka, declared that Yahya Jammeh's government has been overthrown with effect from Tuesday. His statement was supported by Mr. Bamba Mass, a political activist, who maintained that power belongs to the people. Mr. Mass said what happened on Tuesday clearly testified to the fact that this is the beginning of the end of Jammeh's regime. He said they are taking over power and had already occupied the High Commission building.

There was fanfare jubilation around the Gambian High Commission UK offices. The protesters paid tribute to the massacred inmates. They called for an end to Jammeh's one man leadership.

Mrs. Tuku Jallow, a Gambian naturalized United States Citizen, who was on vacation in the UK, said she personally took down Jammeh's pictures from the wall of the High Commission, and tore it apart. She said she was happy to be part of the demonstrators. Tuku said Jammeh's regime has lost the mandate of the Gambian people, and therefore demanded regime change in Banjul.

"I tore Yahya Jammeh's pictures. We have shutdown the Gambian High Commission. We are in control of the High Commission. We have taken over the High Commission. This is our High Commission. Yahya Jammeh's government is history," said Madam Jallow, while denouncing the execution of the nine death row inmates.

Another demonstrator, who did not identify himself, said he also took part in the destruction of dictator Yahya Jammeh's pictures. He publicly insulted Jammeh, and his parents—accusing him of committing genocide in the Gambia. He said he has no regrets for destroying Jammeh's pictures.

Buba Ceesay, who claimed to be part of the leaders of the April 10, 2000, student riots, which left the massacre of 14 unarmed students, was also inside the offices of the High Commission. He denounces dictator Jammeh's leadership, while hailing the protesters for their patriotic move in taking over the High Commission.

Also on the ground was Mr. Abdoulie Jobe, one of the organizers of the demonstration. Both Mr. Jobe and his colleague Malick Kah confirmed that the High Commission had been taken over. They also confirmed that Jammeh's portraits have indeed been vandalized.

Mr. Jobe noted that the taking over of the Gambian Mission signals the end of Jammeh's regime. He said they are committed to dislodging Jammeh from power. Mr. Jobe said Tuesday was a field day for the protesters, as the police could not stop them from manifesting their outrage and anger at the illegal killing of the mile two prison nine inmates.

For Malick Kah, he opined that Tuesday's demonstration was the first of its kind. He noted that they have been organizing protest marches in the UK, but they have never witnessed such a high turnout of protesters in the history of their anti Jammeh protest marches. Mr. Kah then urged the Gambian opposition to compliment the efforts of the Diasporan Community to mount more pressure on the Jammeh dictatorship to respect the fundamental human rights and liberties of Gambians. He callout Hamat Bah's name to please join the Group of 6 opposition leaders to help bail out the country from Jammeh's misrule.

A female speaker denounced the raping of one of the inmates Tabara Samba, a Senegalese, who was repeatedly raped prior to her execution. She described such acts despicably wrong and inhumane. She said dictator Jammeh lacks respect for women, and therefore she appealed to the international community to come to Gambia's aid.

Mr. Seedy Ceesay, the Freedom Radio Anchorman, who covered the demonstrations, said the protesters sat comfortably in the High Commission, and could be heard saying: "We have taken over dictator Yahya Jammeh's regime."

There was nothing the British police could have done to quell the protest, as the protesters said they were at their home. They vandalized Jammeh's pictures and drank tea. The protesters addressed the Gambian nation and the international community inside the High Commission. According to Mr. Ceesay, inside the High Commission, files containing pending passport applications were visible. There was also a piece of paper, in which Yahya Jammeh's name was handwritten, and his phone number.

Mr. Seedy Ceesay also received a phone call on Tuesday afternoon from a caller, who claimed to be one Lt. Mendy. Mendy said he works at the

State House. Mr. Mendy told Mr. Ceesay that he knew his parents. He also warned Seedy not to be part of what was about to happen. Mr. Mendy said they were assigned to go after Pa Nderry's M'Bai parents on Tuesday night. He later hung up the phone.

The protesters did not take any of the High Commission belongings. They said their mission was to communicate to the world and manifest to dictator Jammeh that power belongs to the people. This was repeatedly buttressed by the Gambian Immigration Lawyer Yankuba Darboe. Mr. Darboe said Mr. Jammeh lacks the legitimacy to rule the Gambia. He said the taking over of the High Commission testify to the fact that Gambians are determined to take their country back from the Kanilai monster. Darboe said they have taken over the High Commission and that Jammeh couldn't eject them from the premises. Politician Banoramas also supported Yankuba's statement. He said Jammeh must go!

The protesters wanted to remain inside the High Commission compound for days, but later changed their mind. They spilled uncooked eggs around the doors of the High Commission and inside the High Commission as another form of registering their outrage at the Jammeh status quo before leaving the premises.

The protesters handed a petition documents to the British authorities before meeting with the Deputy Senegalese High Commissioner in the UK. Former Gambian Vice President Bakary Bunja Darboe, who is also a career diplomat, presented the petition to the Senegalese envoy. Mr. Darboe spoke on behalf of the demonstrators, and extended his condolence to the families of the murdered Senegalese nationals, including the Senegalese Government.

The Senegalese envoy welcomed the protesters with an open arm. He said the two countries are one people and he promised to forward the concerns of the marchers to the Senegalese authorities.

Similar protest marches were organized in Georgia, Washington DC, Minnesota, Alaska, Washington state, Rhode Island, and elsewhere around the country. The protesters called for an end to Jammeh's dictatorship.

Meanwhile, due to the Freedom Radio's live coverage of the demonstrations taking place in the United States and in the UK, dictator Jammeh has decided to yank the Internet offline in the Gambia late Tuesday afternoon. A local cellular phone company Qcell in a statement issued on Tuesday said: "Due to maintenance by GAMTEL on the Internet gateway, our data service will be interrupted from 12 am for approximately twenty minutes. We apologize for any inconvenience."

Mr. Jammeh, who is increasingly worried about the global reaction against the killing of the nine inmates, is also contemplating blocking Facebook in the Gambia. He was briefed by his intelligence about the increasing Facebook traffic in the Gambia and its implications to national security.

There are over seven hundred thousand registered Gambian Facebook users back home, and most of the account owners have been voicing their opposition at the killing of the death row inmates. This is evident on their Facebook profile images, in which they completely darkened to register their outrage at the killings.

A Gamtel insider said the dictator has threatened that if they cannot block Facebook, Freedom Newspaper, and HelloGambia, he will then hire someone who can do the job for him. The Freedom Newspaper and HelloGambia have been blocked in the Gambia, but Jammeh said he wants the blockage to be more tightened so that third party websites cannot be used to access both websites. GAMTEL officials are currently faced with such a dilemma. Jammeh wants to censor the Internet.

A successful demonstration was held in Sweden on Friday by the Gambian Community out there—denouncing the illegal execution of the nine death row inmates by Gambia's iron fist President Yahya Jammeh. Gambians across the world have been organizing similar demonstrations calling on dictator Jammeh to step down and hand over the country to credible administration. The Sweden march was a march with a difference. The protesters after storming the streets chanting anti Jammeh slogans, they organized a debate in the evening educating their countrymen about the need for Gambians to remain united and dislodge Jammeh from power. Freedom Radio Anchorman Alhagie Mustapha Faye, alias "alikalagi", Kebba Sanneh, Yaya Dampha, a human rights activist, Ndey Amie Jaw, and other speakers spoke bluntly against Jammeh's misrule.

Ndey Amie Jaw, who identified herself as the daughter of Ajaratu Fatou Kah began her speech by thanking Ambassador Essa Sey, Pa Nderry M'Bai, and Alhagie Mustapha Faye for their excellent role in educating Gambians about Jammeh's misrule. Ndey Amie said it should be the duty of every Gambian to pray for Sey, M'Bai, and Faye for their continued good health. She then shifted her conversation on Jammeh by urging him to stop murdering Gambians at his own accord. Ms. Jaw said Jammeh's rule has brought untold suffering and nightmares for Gambians.

Zang Carroyal, also another speaker said Jammeh's time is up. He said Mr. Jammeh should consider stepping down from power. He said Jammeh has lost the legitimacy to rule the Gambia.

The protesters said the Sweden protest will be an ongoing thing to mount more pressure to end Jammeh's power excesses in the impoverished West African country. This was reechoed by Mr. Kebba Sanneh in his speech, who denounced the execution of the inmates. He branded Yahya Jammeh a non Gambian, who has destroyed the fabric of society in the Gambia. Mr. Sanneh has been a longtime critic of dictator Jammeh. He reminded the audience about his past writings on the pages of the Freedom Newspaper—exposing Jammeh's leadership deficit. Mr. Sanneh used the occasion to inform Jammeh that Gambians will not rest until he is chase out of the State House. He said their preoccupation from now on, is to work towards dislodging Jammeh from power.

"If Jammeh thinks that he can rule this country for billions of years, he must be making the fool of himself. We are determined to take our country back," Mr. Sanneh said while calling on Jammeh to produce the bodies of the murdered inmates. "Jammeh should know that his time is up and we will win. It is victory that we are waiting to win," he added.

For his part Mr. Demba Dem, a former Niani MP for the ruling APRC, who suffered brutal torture in the hands of Jammeh's agents after he was accused of being complicit in a coup plot back in 2006, hailed Ms. Jaw for her passionate speech. Mr. Dem hailed Gambian women for responding positively during the march. He said Jammeh must go, and there is no turning back on the struggle.

The main man behind the protest Alhagie Mustapha Faye spoke briefly in the local Aku language before speaking in his native wollof language to expose Jammeh's crimes against humanity. Mr. Faye also spoke about Jammeh's hatred against women folks. He said the late Tabara Samba, one of the Senegalese inmates executed in the Gambia had her breast and tongue cutoff by Jammeh's agents before she was killed. He accused Mr. Jammeh of committing genocide and crimes against humanity. He said the Senegalese government should take up the issue with the Jammeh regime so that justice is seen to be done in the case of their murdered nationals by the Kanilai monster.

Applauded by a cheering crowd, Faye reminded the gathering that a criminal complaint has been filed against Yahya Jammeh in the Hague by concerned Gambians affected by Jammeh's terror. He said the efforts to uproot Jammeh from power is not negotiable adding that no amount of threats can make Gambians to quit the struggle. Faye said Yahya Jammeh has not only been committing crimes against our people, but he has been using the office of the presidency for his own economic gains. He accused Yahya Jammeh of pocketing millions of dollars aid money belonging to Gambians. His statement was greeted with an applause by the gathering who chanted "down with Jammeh. Down with Jammeh."

He said Jammeh has been the main sponsor of the former Senegalese President Abdoulie Wade. He accused the Kanilai monster of using Gambian taxpayers funds to sponsor Wade's past election programs in Senegal. "By hook, or by crook, we will get this man out of the Presidency," Faye said.

CHAPTER SIX

EDITOR M'BAI'S LONDON MAIDEN SPEECH

In July of 2012, I visited my colleague Sheriff Seedy Ceesay in the United Kingdom. Mr. Ceesay lives in Brighton with his family. During my trip, I was accorded with the opportunity to address a meeting in Camden, where some Freedom Newspaper and Radio fans converged to witness my maiden speech. The London trip also avail me with the opportunity to reunite with family members, colleagues in the media, and my fans. It was a successful trip. I also took pictures with my fans. Below is full text of my London speech . . . .

Delivered On Saturday July 14th 2012

By Pa Nderry M'Bai

Author's E-mail: panderrymbai@gmail.com

Good evening London. It's a great pleasure, and delight to be part of a historic gathering—the first of its kind here in the great city of Camden in the United Kingdom. I am exceedingly happy tonight to have a face-to face dialogue with the Freedom Newspaper/Freedom Radio fans within and outside the UK.

Before going further, I want to ask the following questions: Is there anyone here from the Gambian High Commission in London? If there is someone from the London Gambian High Commission, please let the person raises his or her hand up. I have an important message to deliver to President Jammeh. Relax, and chill. Feel at home. We want you to communicate accurately to President Jammeh about what is being discussed here. This is an important forum, which will no doubt determine the future of Gambia's destiny.

Is there anyone in this gathering representing the National Intelligence Agency, the (NIA)? If you are from the NIA, you do not need to raise your hand. We will excuse the individual from blowing his, or her cover—given the risk associated with your job, and the privacy governing the intelligence tradecraft. Is there anyone in this forum supporting Yaya Jammeh and his APRC Party? Please raise your hand? Please listen to me carefully, and you will learn how Yaya Jammeh is steadily destroying and dividing our country, as a nation.

Once again, I want to emphasize that I feel honored and privileged to be availed with the opportunity to address this great gathering. Since I landed in the UK, Gambians and non-Gambians from all the corners of the UK have been calling to say "Pa Nderry welcome to the UK."

My phone kept ringing round the clock, as people phoned to express their delight, and pleasure in having me in this great country. These fine and patriotic callers acknowledged what they called the "brilliant job" the Freedom Newspaper and Freedom Radio staffers are doing in educating Gambians about the activities of the "mafia" regime in Banjul, which is hell bent on undermining the basic liberties and freedoms of Gambians.

Some of these callers even personally invited me to their homes to meet their wonderful families, friends, and neighbors. We want to salute the Gambian Community in the UK for according us such a kind reception and hospitality.

I also want extend my sincere thanks, and appreciation to my colleague Seedy Ceesay, and his wonderful family for taking good care of me during my trip. I have enjoyed the finest hospitality in Ceesay's home. Food and drinks were in abundance. I sometimes even feel being overfed by Seedy and his family. No kidding. I am dead serious. Abaraka Seedy and the family for the kind treatment extended to me.

The London meeting, is basically aimed among other things: shaping the future of our beloved nation the Gambia, under the bankrupt leadership of despot Yaya Jammeh, educating our people about the urgency to reclaim our country from Gambia's visionless leader, restoring freedom, and human rights in the Gambia, public empowerment through mass media campaign education, the restoration of our country's lost and most cherished political, religious, traditional, and cultural values.

Under Jammeh's rule, we have lost all our fine values. Freedom is alien to Gambians under Jammeh's watch! Human right is alien to Gambians. The Gambia is a country, where impunity rules. He has transformed the country as his personal property. Jammeh owns virtually every sector of our economy.

The London meeting will also prepare Gambians for post Jammeh era, as political change is inevitable in the Gambia. The writings are already on the wall for a regime change.

Gambians should start bracing up for the ardent task on their way in rebuilding their country. Dictator Jammeh, and his cronies have perpetrated so much harm, destruction, and economic mismanagement in a span of 18 years against our country.

The economic mess, and damage perpetrated by Jammeh, and his Lebanese Hezbollah supporters so called investors partners in Banjul is irreparable. It will take Gambians generations to rebuild this onetime great nation called the "smiling coast of West Africa."

The Gambia under Jammeh's misguided leadership has been transformed as a drug hub nation, an avenue for money laundering, state organized crime syndicate, and disappearances of political opponents.

The Gambia is no longer the Promised Land. Our people are among the most economically disadvantaged people in the sub-region. There is hopelessness, fear, economic stagnation, and destitution in the Gambia.

In The Gambia, there is no participatory democracy, no press freedom, no government accountability, and no sound institutions to manage the affairs of the nation. Institutionalized corruption is the order of the day under Jammeh's rule. The regime is not making any serious efforts in combating official graft, discrimination, and nepotism. There is a growing culture of corruption in Jammeh's regime.

Development has been hindered in The Gambia largely due to bureaucracy. There are square pegs in round holes (novices) entrusted with key positions in government, who do not have the experience, expertise, and knowledge to execute such functions.

For Mr. Jammeh, qualification is insignificant in his government. What matters to Jammeh is: how much an individual is loyal to the status quo, including his humble self. That's why the country has today emerged as a failed state.

There is no functional government in the Gambia, as we speak tonight brother and sisters. The leadership is DEAD, the infrastructure, and the economy have collapsed, no human resources, the private sector, which is the country's main economic backbone is DEAD, Gambia's Gross Domestic Product, (GDP)) is not the best in the sub-region. Our GDP has been performing badly in recent times. Tourism is gone! There is no high spending tourists coming to the Gambia. There is no direct Foreign Investment—thanks to dictator Jammeh's misplaced economic priorities.

No serious investor wants to invest in the Gambia. Investors are not assured of the safety, and the security of their investments. For this to happen, there must be strong, and independent legal framework put in place to safeguard genuine and honest investment in the Gambia.

But unfortunately, there is no independent, credible, and reliable judiciary that should serve as a neutral arbitrator during investment disputes, and other legal matters affecting local citizens.

The Gambian judiciary belongs to dictator Jammeh. He has repeatedly interfered with the day-to-day operations of the judiciary. Judges have been arrested, detained, and sacked without reasons. The Gambian populace has lost faith in their own judiciary—thanks to Jammeh's meddling into the affairs of this important arm of government. The average Gambian does not have faith in the judiciary.

That said, let shift our gears to the area of press freedom and human rights. We have lost fine men and women during the 18 years struggle along the road in our attempt to reclaim our country from the Kanilai monster.

Please join me in paying a special tribute to the late Managing Editor, and Publisher of the Point Newspaper Deyda Hydra. May Mr. Hydra's soul rest in perfect peace. We picked up the fight from where Mr. Hydra stops—we mean on the day of his brutal murder by the criminal government of Yaya Jammeh. We will defeat Hydara's killers God willing. There will be no retreat, no surrender in our quest to make the Gambia a better country, in which its citizens will feel proud to be associated with it.

As we converged here in London, let us also pay tribute to the late Gambian journalist Pa Omar Barrow, and the 14 unarmed school children, who were murdered in April of 2000 by Yaya Jammeh's thugs. This was the darkest day in Gambian history. This was the day, when our sons and daughters were gun down in broad daylight for merely demanding justice in the case of their colleague Ebrima Barry, who was tortured to death by the personnel of the Brikama Fire, and Ambulance Services. Dozens of other students were maimed in that incident, some of whom are still recovering from that bloody incident.

We cannot wrap up this program, without paying tribute to the fallen members of the Gambia Armed Forces, some of whom had risked their lives in trying to end the Jammeh misrule, and in the process were summarily executed by the dictator. Our prayers are with the late Lt. Abdoulie Faal, AKA DOT Faal, Captain Basiru Barrow, Lt. Saye, just to name a few.

To the current leadership of the Gambia Armed Forces, we say remain focus, be patriotic, stick to your oath of allegiance to the constitution, and recognize the fact that you are duty bound to protect Gambians from Jammeh's aggression, power abuses, and economic monopoly.

Mr. Jammeh is not concerned about a professional army. If he does, he will not be misusing power as a Commander-in-Chief: to falsely frame our men and women in uniform, prematurely retiring them from the army, falsely prosecuting them on a trumped up coup charges, employing the "DIVIDE AND RULE" card to sow seeds of discord amongst the rank and file of the army hierarchy.

Admitted, or not, there is no officer today in the Gambia Armed Forces who is safe from Jammeh's power abuse. The staff turnover in the army (I mean the number of soldiers and officers being fired without reasons) is the highest in the sub-region.

Like all other institutions, The Gambian army has also been politicized by Jammeh. Soldiers are not rewarded based on their competence, hard work, merit, professionalism, and dedication to national duty. Instead, Jammeh appreciates soldiers, who are willing to lie for him, harm Gambians, and disadvantaged their other hardworking comrades.

The onus now lies on the genuine members of The Gambia Armed Forces to recognize the fact that the status quo in Banjul is no longer sustainable. We cannot afford to have a leadership that's discriminatory against its own people, inept, incompetent, and lacks the vision to steer the affairs of the nation.

It should be incumbent upon every peace loving Gambian, including members of The Gambian Armed Forces to galvanize their resources, and efforts to make the supreme sacrifice to bailout our country from Jammeh's misrule. The time has come to take charge of your own country. Thanks for your attention.

Signed: Pa Nderry M'Bai
Managing Editor/Publisher Freedom Newspaper, INC,
Raleigh, North Carolina
E-Mail: panderrymbai@gmail.com
Tel: 001-919-749-6319

CHAPTER SEVEN

EDITOR M'BAI JULY 22ND MILITARY TAKEOVER MAIDEN SPEECH

Dated Tuesday July 24th 2012

Good morning Gambia:

In the name of Allah, the merciful, and the most benevolent, I say Ramadan Mubarak to the Muslim Umma. May by God's divine intervention and willing, next year by this time, dictator Jammeh, and his criminal regime will be history!

Our nation has just witnessed another eighteen years of dictator Yaya Jammeh's misrule. Eighteen years of economic stagnation! Eighteen years of political oppression. Eighteen years of economic hardship. Eighteen years of misplaced economic priorities. Eighteen years of reign of terror against our people. Eighteen years of culture of corruption under Jammeh's rule.

Brothers and Sisters, the road to Gambia's political freedom will be a daunting one, but we will surely get there. Many lives have been lost along the road in our eighteen years struggle to dislodge a mafia regime headed by an internationally busted drug and arms dealer in the person of Yaya Jammeh.

Brothers and Sisters, we owe it to our fallen men and women of the struggle to keep up with the fight until victory is ours. We must take back our country from these bandits calling themselves rulers.

Eighteen years of Jammeh's rule has deprived our people both economic, and political empowerment. The Gambia is no longer the Promised Land. This country has been transformed as a failed state—thanks dictator Jammeh's lack of foresight, political maturity, and good leadership to steer the affairs of our beloved nation—called the Gambia.

Brothers and Sisters, in order to restore our lost political values, and freedoms as a nation, there must be a united front to bailout our country from the clutches of Jammeh's one man rule. Unity is a MUST, if we truly want to emancipate the Gambia from despotism!

Power belongs to the people. Freedom never comes under silver-plata. We must emulate other freedom loving nations, who risked their lives on the course of fighting for the freedoms, and liberties of their people. If Libyans can do it, why not Gambia? If Egypt can do it, why not tiny Gambia? If Tunisia can do it, why not Gambia?

Dating back to Western civilization, post Western independence, great nations such as the United States of America, France, Germany, and elsewhere around Europe fought for their people's freedoms, and national sovereignty. Gambians must fight for their own freedom and liberties.

Freedom goes with a price. Our people must be ready, and committed in fighting for what they believe in. Gambia's freedom is not negotiable. We must take back our country from Jammeh's criminal mafia regime. This regime doesn't represent the interest and future of Gambians.

In this modern day and age, (I mean the 21st century), the Gambia is one of the few countries in Africa condoning a visionless leader like Yahya Jammeh. The silence on the side of our people to end the rule of fear is unacceptable. Our people should man up, and stand up against a criminal regime. Now is the time to stand up to be counted Gambia!

The diasporan Gambian community could play an important role in spearheading a revolution back home. A revolution that will wipe the tears of our suffering countrymen. A revolution that will put an end to nepotism, one man rule, and gross rights abuses!

Ladies and Gentlemen, Gambians in the diaspora should not under any given circumstances underestimate their influence in shaping the affairs of our nation. You represent a politically starve nation. You represent an economically bankrupt nation. You represent the future of the Gambia. I say rise up Gambia to reclaim your robbed nation from Jammeh.

What is needed now; is the consolidation, and the galvanization of our collective efforts in dislodging the Kanilai monster. No single person can mount a successful revolution. Revolution requires sense of purpose, unity, solidarity, and commitment. Unity is our strength Gambia! Let us unite for the sake of reclaiming our country from a mafia regime.

To the members of Gambia Armed Forces, we are aware of the trials, and tribulations that you are going through at this hour. But you got to realize that without a free country, there cannot be a professional army. Without a free country, there cannot be justice and fair-play, without a free country, there cannot be an independent press, without a free country, there cannot be rule of law. We therefore indulge you to join progressive Gambians in reclaiming our country.

Let no one fools you that Jammeh will represent your interest. He is on the other hand undermining the wellbeing of the army. Gambia's army represents Jammeh's interest, and not the collective interest of Gambians. He has reduced the army as a political tool, which he uses to perpetrate all kinds of crimes against our people.

In a span of eighteen years, Jammeh has fired more than four army chiefs without any form of resistance, or resentment on the side of the army hierarchy to denounce his politicization of the military.

From CDS Babourcarr Jatta, Lang Tombong Tamba, Ndure Cham, and of recent Masaneh Kinteh, all have been fired without anyone standing up against Jammeh's power abuses!

Gambia will never forgive our army for not acting at a time when they are most needed in our country's history. The Gambian military should recognize that standing up against Jammeh's power abuses is not only a moral obligation, but a constitutional requirement.

It's legitimate for the Gambian army to protect Gambians from any form of aggression—be it domestic or external one. And Jammeh has over the years exposed our people to the reign of terror!

Finally, brothers and Sisters, there is light at the end of the tunnel. We will emerge victorious at the end of the day. Gambians will one day emerge from Jammeh's tyranny. God bless the Gambia and her people.

CHAPTER EIGHT

WHO IS PRESIDENT YAHYA JAMMEH?

Like many rural boys, Gambian dictator Yahya Jammeh too has his own story to tell to the world. But unfortunately, the African despot is not opening up about his life story. Perhaps, Mr. Jammeh has something to hide to Gambians and the world: His background as a child growing up in a poor family setting and his rebellious tendencies as a child. His Dad Abdul Aziz James Junkung Jammeh was a career wrestler. And his Mum Madam Asombi Bojang was a housewife, cum petty trader. Jammeh's grandparents migrated to the Gambia from neighboring Casamance. Mr. Jammeh was reported to have been born in a small village called Kanilai. Although, there is a big question mark surrounding Jammeh's Gambian citizenship, but our sources maintained that Jammeh is a Gambian despite the controversy associated with his citizenship.

Alhagie Boto Colley, a resident of Jeshwang, but originally from Bwiam Kankuntu helped Yahya Jammeh to secure his birth certificate, when he (Boto Colley) used to work at the Medical and Health Department as a Storekeeper. Mr. Colley, was very supportive to Yahya Jammeh. He used to provide Jammeh with lunch money, bed sheet, clothing, and medication if he (Jammeh) or his mum were sick. Other Foni natives can also attest to the fact that Mr. Boto Colley has always been there for them during the First Republic. Boto was the Chief Storekeeper at the Medical and Health Department. He has access to medicine, and other health information that he uses to help his people. He is running one of Yahya Jammeh's business outlets around Jimpex in Kanifing. He is some kind of a Store Manager. He sells rice, sugar, cement, oil, and building materials for Jammeh.

Mr. Jammeh's late father Junkung Jammeh was a non believer. He doesn't believe in God. At the time, the Muslim faith was never practiced in Kanilai. Christian missionaries mainly from Ireland, and elsewhere around Europe came to Kanilai to baptize residents and also dug a well for the village. Kanilai primary school stops at grade five at the time. That was one of the reasons why Yahya Jammeh had to move from Kanilai to Bwiam's Saint Edwards Primary school to complete his primary education. He repeated grade five in Bwiam before sitting to the grade six Common Entrance Examinations.

Mr. Jammeh won a government scholarship when he sat for the Common Entrance. Out of over three hundred students, he emerged third in the entire school. Maharr Ceesay, the daughter of a Bwiam businessman took first and her sister Fatou Ceesay emerged second. Alhagie Babou Ceesay of Bwiam is the father of the Ceesay sisters. Mamharr works at the Treasury Department, while her sister Fatou Ceesay used to work for the Action Aid the Gambia.

Mr. Jammeh's Dad shared the same Mum and Dad with the late Jayjaw Jammeh of Kanilai. Jayjaw Jammeh was a traditional healer, who specialized in curing fractured legs and other ailments. Jayjaw hailed from the Kanilai Jammeh family. He is related to the parents of Pa Harry Jammeh, Gambia's Solicitor General. Pa Harry's father is the late John Jammeh, a retired Gambian educationist. Mr. John Jammeh used to be a Headmaster at the Saint Edwards Primary school in Bwiam, while Pa Harry's Mum Susan Kujabi, is a school teacher. Mr. Jammeh financed Pa Harry's law degree in the United Kingdom.

Pa Harry's father John Jammeh, Yahya Jammeh's Father Junkung Jammeh, and that of Ben Jammeh's father are related. The trio, are close relatives. They are biologically related. Pa Harry is second in command at Gambia's Justice Department, while Ben Jammeh is in charge of Gambia's anti narcotic unit. The President has annexed the National Drug Enforcement Agency (NDEA) under his office. The NDEA reports directly to Jammeh. This came in the wake of the seizure of one billion dollars of street value of cocaine in the Gambia. South American nationals granted investment license by the government to fish in the Gambia were blamed for the drug presence in the West African country.

Yahya Jammeh was a baptized Catholic. His Christian name was James Jammeh. Father MacDonald, an Irish priest baptized Mr. Jammeh into the Christian faith. Father MacDonald played an important role towards Yahya Jammeh's life as a youngster. That was one of the reasons why when Jammeh seized power from the former Gambian President Sir Dawda Kairaba Jawara, he had to travel to Ireland to meet with father MacDonald during the Commonwealth Summit. He was in Ireland on an official trip, but that doesn't stop Jammeh from paying a visit to his Godfather. He owed a special gratitude to Father MacDonald because this was the guy, who helped to shape his life as youngster growing in an economically disadvantaged family.

Father MacDonald, Father Moore, and Father Grind were the first Christian missionaries assigned to Bwiam. Yahya Jammeh was among the Kanilai kids baptized by the Western priest. Among them was Benedict Jammeh, the current Director General of the National Drug Enforcement Agency. Ben was going to school in Bwiam with Yahya Jammeh. He goes with the aliases Lambandeh. Ben Jammeh briefly left the Gambia for Liberia with Pa Harry's uncle Peter Kujabi some years ago to study to become a priest. Ben's guardian in Bwiam was Honorable Aba Sanyang's father. Aba Sanyang used to be an APRC Parliamentarian. He was recently appointed Gambia's Deputy Chief of Mission in Cuba. Aba's mother Isatou Darammeh, widely known as Ma Drammeh was Ben Jammeh's guardian in Bwiam as well. Ma Drammeh is an aunty to Yankuba Drammeh, the former Deputy Chief of Defense Staff of Gambia's Armed Forces. Mr. Drammeh is currently working at the Gambian Mission at the United Nations in New York.

The Catholic Mission in Bwiam helps poor students like Yahya Jammeh with food and clothing. Father MacDonald and his team used to tour the locality to provide free food to starving Foni communities. At the time, there was no clean drinking water in Kanilai. Villagers fetched water from nearby ponds in the outskirt of the village. Thanks to Father MacDonald, Moore and Grind, well water was made accessible to the villagers of Kanilai.

As a child attending primary education in Bwiam, Yahya Jammeh experienced numerous challenges. His parents entrusted him to one

Henry Jammeh, a former teacher at the Saint Augustine's High School, who is a native of Kanilai. Henry later resettled in Bwiam, where he bought a house. Henry's Dad and that of Yahya Jammeh's Dad are related. Henry Jammeh used to teach Math, Physics, and Chemistry. His responsibility was to play the role of a father figure and a responsible host for Yahya Jammeh. He was tasked to look after poor Yahya Jammeh. Jammeh's feeding, and accommodation was under Henry Jammeh's responsibility. For some unknown reasons, Henry Jammeh couldn't get along with Yahya Jammeh, who is Gambia's President today. Henry had to kick out Jammeh from his home and asked him to find a new guardian. Jammeh was a treble kid, who was hard to maintain. He hardly heeds to parental advice. He does things on his own way. He was yanked out of Henry Jammeh's home in Bwiam. His parents had to travel to Bwiam to look for a new host for him.

The late John P Bojang, the former Headmaster of Saint Edwards Primary school of Buwiam was approached by Jammeh's parents to consider hosting their kicked out child and he agreed. Mr. John P Bojang and Jammeh's mother Asombi Bojang came from the same family home. He is related to Asombi Bojang. Mr. Bojang has family ties in Bajana and Kaimo villages in Foni. He lived in Kombo Lamin before his unfortunate death. That was one of the reasons why Jammeh appointed him as a Minister, and later Gambia's Ambassador to the United States of America. Mr. Bojang helped to look after Jammeh, when he was going to school in Bwiam. Unfortunately, John P Bojang and Jammeh couldn't get along as well. Mr. Jammeh exhibited the same stubborn behavior while under the guardianship of Mr. Bojang. He was asked to leave the house since learning to listen to one's elders was not part of his upbringing as a child.

After he was kicked out by John P Bojang, Jammeh's parents this time around approached one Getala Tamba to help supervise their son while he was going to school in Bwiam. Getala Tamba is the father of Wuiyai Tamba, a former Fire officer now residing in England. Getala is a tailor by profession. At the time, the late Lebatch Bojang, and his brother Amadi Bojang were hosted by the old man alongside with Yahya Jammeh. Amadi Bojang works at the Kanilai Fire Department. His brother Lebatch Bojang died in the United States of America some years ago. Yahya Jammeh personally financed the airlifting of Lebatch's body, and burial expenses. Jammeh, Lebatch, and Amadi Bojang are close first cousins. They were hosted by Getala Tamba while they were going to school in Bwaim. Jammeh's stay at Getala's home was short-lived due to his inability to farm. Yahya was skinny, malnourished at the time, and could hardly farm. Getala Tamba held the view that it was a waste of time to feed a lazy child like Jammeh since he was not contributing in the house in the form of farming. Getala allowed Lebatch, and his brother Amadi to stay at his home, but insisted that Jammeh must find a new guardian. This was how Jammeh was yanked out of Getala's home.

Jammeh's parents again reach out to one Manjai Sanyang to help oversee their child while he goes to school in Bwiam. Manjai Sanyang used to reside in Bwiam Kankuntu. He earns his living as a watchman. He was stationed at the Bwiam Agric groundnut depot. His job was to protect the groundnut depot. Manjai agreed to look after Jammeh. He was very supportive to Yahya Jammeh. Occasionally, he will give lunch money to Jammeh. Jammeh used to spend time with him at his work place at night. Jammeh's late night visits to his host Manjai was basically motivated by his sheer greed for groundnut consumption and to get lunch money from the old man the next day for school. Mr. Jammeh stayed at the home of Manjai Sanyang until his demise, before he was moved to another guardian in Dobong. In fact, one Bubai Sanyang, a former police officer is a close relative of Manjai Sanyang. Bubai was posted at Faraffeni, and his last posting was Kalagi police station before his retirement from the Force. He later worked for President Jammeh serving as one of his business Managers in Bwiam together with Ndongo Mboob. Both Sanyang and Mboob were tasked to sell Jammeh's rice, sugar, oil, and onions to the local populace. They later fell out with Jammeh after been accused of financial embezzlement. Bubai Sanyang and Ndongo Mboob, both natives of Bwiam have been feared dead. They have been missing for years. Reports have it that the Kanilai dictator murdered them and dumped their remains at his crocodile pool in Kanilai. The missing detainees left families behind. Ndongo Mboob was never married. Bubai Sanyang and Alhagie Boto Colley are first cousins. Jammeh turn around and killed Bubai Sanyang, and now Bubai's cousin Boto is working for Jammeh.

In Dobong, Babai Gibba became his parental guardian. Babai Gibba is the father of Momodou Lamin Gibba, the former Managing Director of the Social Security Housing Finance Corporation. Mr. Gibba is the current Managing Director of the Gambia Ports Authority. He goes with the aliases Goro Gibba. Both Goro Gibba and Jammeh were raised by Babai Gibba. Jammeh used to commute to school on foot from Dobong to Buwiam. Goro Gibba is one of the most educated folks in Dobong. He had an MBA from a London University. After his graduation, he returned to the Gambia. He was on the verge of securing a high paying job with the then new owners of the Kairaba Beach Hotel, but Jammeh decided that he should work for his government. Jammeh sent his emissaries: the Kujabi brothers asking Mr. ML Gibba to reconsider his decision and accept a job offer from the President to head the Asset Management Recovery Corporation (APRC). But Mr. Gibba was still defiant. He said he wanted to work for the hotel. Abdoulie Kujabi, the former head of the National Intelligence Agency had to step in to inform Gibba that he either accepts the President's offer, or he might risk losing employment opportunities in the Gambia. Gibba complied and was appointed the Managing Director of the AMRC. Kawsu Gibba, the former Member of Parliament for Bwiam and also the Managing Director of the defunct Continent Bank is a close relative of Goro Gibba. Kawsu had problems with Jammeh in the wake of the Continent Bank bankruptcy. The two later reconciled their differences.

Mr. Kawsu Gibba was recently appointed member of Gambia's Judicial Service Commission, alongside with businessman Amadou Samba and lawyer Pa Badou Conteh. Mr. Conteh represented Gumbo Touray during his trial. Touray was charged with giving false information to a public officer. His case was dismissed due to lack of evidence. His attorney Pa Badou Conteh got appointed by the State to serve as a member of the Judicial Service Commission while Gumbo Touray's case was pending in court. Weekes later, Mr. Touray was freed by the court. The court also ruled that the academic credentials of the Vice Chancellor of the University of the Gambia, Professor Muhammed Kah should be reviewed to establish as to whether he (Kah) was fit to head the nation's highest learning institution.

While in Dobong under the guardianship of Babai Gibba, Jammeh was hosted in a tiny room. He doesn't have a mattress to sleep on. He slept on a locally made mattress filled with grasses. His room was infested with bedbugs. Poor Jammeh had only one set of uniform to put on for weeks to go to school in Bwiam. His plight was so miserable. Jammeh's survives on handouts from benevolent neighbors and Christian missionaries posted in Bwiam.

The likes of Alhagie Mustapha James Kujabi, and Omar Gibba, Gambia's Ambassador to Cuba were Jammeh's childhood friends in Dobong. Omar Gibba is a former school teacher. It was James Kujabi, who facilitated Omar Gibba's appointment into Jammeh's regime. Sulayman Masanneh Ceesay was the head of the Personnel Management office (PMO) at the time. Mr. Gibba is a graduate of the University of the Gambia. Thanks to James Kujabi, he quits his teaching job to join the State House Protocol team. He started as an Assistant Secretary before rising to the ranks. Mr. Yahya Jammeh was always been in the company of James Kujabi and Omar Gibba. They hang out together in the neighborhood in Dobong. James Kujabi's late brother Jasaja Kujabi, a man gifted with spiritual knowledge also played a pivotal role towards Jammeh's upbringing as an impoverished child in Dobong. Mr. Jammeh amassed most of his "jujus" from Jasaja Kujabi. Jasaja used to be a truck driver for Alhagie Babou Ceesay of Bwiam. Mr. Jammeh allegedly ordered for Jasaja's murder, following a dispute between the two over the detention of his brother James Kujabi. Dictator Jammeh was not the least happy about Jasaja's move to confront him about the arrest and subsequent detention of his brother James Kujabi.

Mr. James Kujabi's problems with Jammeh started when the dictator falsely accused him and one Malafi Sanyang, a former police officer of car theft. Mr. Kujabi was a Protocol officer at the State House at the time, while Malafi Sanyang, was a police traffic officer attached to the State House. Mr. Sanyang later died in jail after he was found guilty by a Gambian court on corruption related charges.

This author interviewed James Kujabi in the wake of the car theft allegations and he categorically denied the allegations. Kujabi's rebuttal of the allegations was a front page story in the Point Newspaper, where

I used to work as a senior staff reporter before migrating to the United States. President Jammeh frowned at James Kujabi's move to talk to the Point Newspaper after confronting him about the Point reportage of the story. Mr. Jammeh even queried as to why James should talk to his enemies—referring to the Point Newspaper. Months later, James Kujabi, was arrested and detained by the NIA for about eighty days. He left the Gambia for the United States shortly after his release.

The Late Deyda Hydara, the Managing Editor of the Point Newspaper confided to me prior to the publication of James Kujabi's reaction to our story expressing concern if Mr. Kujabi will not be in trouble for speaking to the Point. Hydara's concerns were very legitimate. Jammeh's hostile reaction after the publication of our story was a clear testimony to Hydara's reservations about the implications of publishing the story.

As a young man, Mr. Jammeh was very ambitious. He engaged in petty business to earn a living while going to school in Bwiam. Occasionally, he will fetch firewood in the bushes of Dobong and sell it to find some lunch money for school, and other educational expenses. Mr. Jammeh was also in the business of climbing palm trees to look for palm tree nuts locally known in wollof dialect as "Knewlu." He in turn sells the palm tree nuts to neighbors.

Also part of Jammeh's fundraising drive, was his growing interest in harvesting people's mangos. He allegedly intruded into people's mango farms and stole their mangoes. Jammeh would bring the stolen mango in school and sell it to his fellow students. There is also what they called "bush cassava" in Buwiam. Jammeh likes bush cassava. It is his favorite meal. He spent hours in the bush in search of bush cassava. He eats some part of the cassava and the rest he will sell it. Jammeh was also in the business of selling fresh boiled peanuts and a local Gambian fruit called Kaba.

Within Dobong, and its surrounding villages, Mr. Jammeh was known to be walking barefooted. He was often called the barefoot man. He was a rough child, but full of ambition. His favorite shoe color was a green "slipass." That's where his ruling party's color originates. Jammeh has always been obsessed with green colors. There was also what they called "pademnjeyen." It's a traditional Gambian made shoe. Jammeh was occasionally seen walking with such shoes. He never had a girlfriend while in Bwiam and Dobong.

As Jammeh is busy mystifying himself to Gambians, claiming to be a devoted Muslim, walking around with the Holy Koran, it's imperative to note that Mr. Jammeh was baptized as a Christian by Father MacDonald of the Bwiam Christian Mission. Jammeh used to drink the locally made Gambian palm wine called in the Jolla dialect "Bunaka." Jammeh also used to eat pork.

While in Dobong, Jammeh used to hang around Bwiam with other Dobong boys to buy fish from one Dembo Bojang of Gunjur. Mr. Bojang used to drive an old Landover at the time. Poor kids like Yahya Jammeh were often sent by their guardians to buy fish from fishmonger Dembo Bojang.

When I first talked about Jammeh's childhood days in Bwiam and Dobong, on my Freedom Radio weekly show, the agents of the National Intelligence Agency (NIA) assigned to monitor Freedom Radio broadcast materials recorded the show, and transcribed what I said in the local Wollof dialect into English. The President was briefed by the NIA, and he in turn summons Benedict Jammeh and Pa Harry Jammeh, expressing outrage as to who must have been the main source of my radio program. Mr. Jammeh told the Jammeh brothers that someone who must have known him very well during his teenage days in Bwiam must have leaked the story to my humble self Pa Nderry M'Bai. Mr. Jammeh then said to Ben and Pa Harry that he has someone in mind whom he suspects to have spoken to me about his past village life. President Jammeh also instructed Ben and Pa Harry to consult some Bwiam natives residing overseas to confront them about the information reported by the Freedom Radio Anchorman Pa Nderry M'Bai.

Both Pa Harry and Ben Jammeh placed some phone calls overseas. Some of the people they contacted in the West denied communicating with the Freedom Newspaper Editor. Pa Harry in particular confronted one Bwiam native, resident in the United Kingdom, and he informed him that President Jammeh has assigned them to investigate about the person who must have leaked the story about Jammeh's childhood days in Bwiam and Dobong to the Freedom Editor. According to sources, Pa Harry told the Bwiam native that President Jammeh is very upset and he (Yahya Jammeh) wanted to get to the bottom of the story—to find out about the individual leaking what he considered as his "childhood secrets" to the Freedom Newspaper. Mr. Benedict Jammeh also passed Jammeh's message to the Bwiam native, who is on President Jammeh's list of suspected Freedom Newspaper informants discussing his secrets with this author. The folks contacted by Ben and Pa Harry emphatically denied having affiliation with the Freedom Editor. Some of the folks contacted told the Jammeh brothers that they do not have the time to castigate, or discuss President Jammeh's private life as a village teenager. They also told Ben and Pa Harrry that they were busy going to work and taking care of their families.

President Jammeh has concluded that a certain Bwiam native residing overseas was the main source of the Freedom Radio program revelation. Mr. Jammeh told Ben and Pa Harry that there is nobody in Bwiam, besides the person in question who is so knowledgeable about his childhood days.

Meanwhile, both Pa Harry and Ben have launched an appeal to the folks on Jammeh's list of suspected Freedom Newspaper informants to desist from discussing the President's childhood life with this author. The consequences for such activities are dire, the Jammeh brothers told the Bwiam natives they called on the phone. The Jammeh brothers also couldn't understand why should anyone with his right state of mind from Foni calling him, or herself a true Jolla, who supports, or love the Gambian President will discuss President Jammeh's secrets with a person they perceived as an arch encmy of President Jammeh. Ben and Pa Harry said they want folks supplying information to Editor Pa Nderry M'Bai about Mr. Jammeh's childhood life to stop, otherwise they might regret their actions.

Next, we look into Jammeh's "Jollanization" of his government. Since coming to power through a coup, Yahya Jammeh has been steadily consolidating himself into power. He surrounded himself with his ethnic group—the Jollas. Almost all the key positions in government are manned by Jammeh's ethnic group. Mr. Jammeh came from a minority ethnic group. He thinks that the best way to further consolidate himself into power is to empower his own people.

In a span of eighteen years of his rule, Mr. Jammeh has ensured that the Gambian Jolla Community, who used to do low class jobs in the Gambia, acquired University education and other important portfolios in his regime. This is evident on the composition of his administration. Below is a breakdown of the number of Jollas manning key positions in Jammeh's government. Without any prejudice, some of the listed folks are highly educated, but the issue of ethnic diversity is alien to Yahya Jammeh. Mr. Jammeh hides under the banner of fighting tribalism in the Gambia, but the reality is that Yahya Jammeh is a tribalist. The list goes like this:

Abdou Kolley, Minister of Finance and Economic Affairs.

Amadou Colley, the Governor of the Central Bank of the Gambia

Fatim Badjie, Minister of Health and Social Welfare

Ousman Sonko, Minister of Interior

Numo Kujabi, The Director General of the National Intelligence Agency

Benedict Jammeh, the Director General of the National Drug Enforcement Agency

Ousman Badjie, the Chief of Defense Staff of The Gambia Armed Forces

Lieutenant Colonel Lamin Sanneh, Commander of the State Guard Battalion

Momodou Lamin Gibba, the Managing Director of The Gambia Ports Authority

Baboucarr Sanyang, the Managing Director of GAMTEL

Saikou Kujabi, the Managing Director of the Asset Management Recovery Commission

Momodou Sanyang, the Director General of The Gambia Radio and Television Services

There are other institutions headed by Jollas. The Governor of the Central Bank of the Gambia Amadou Colley came from Bwiam Sanchaba. Mr. Jammeh has a vested interest in most of his appointees. Some of his employees are either his former childhood friends in Buwiam, Dobong, relatives, or ethnic tribesmen.

The "Jollanization" of the Gambia Government has undermined national development. There are square pegs in round holes running the affairs of the nation. It's across the board. Almost every sector of the Gambian economy has been grossly affected by Jammeh's ethnic monopoly of our beloved country the Gambia.

In the Army, the majority of unit heads come from the Jolla minority ethnic background. Some of the folks running these units are not very conversant with the work of the military. School dropouts are heading units in the army, police and the NIA. This to some extent has undermined Gambia's national security. The country's security and that of the President is entrusted to novice with barely any security knowledge. They can barely process, or analyze intelligence from any serious intelligence security outfit. There are pros and cons associated with the security ramifications about Jammeh's "Jollanization" of Gambia's workforce. In the short term, Jammeh will reap the benefits of his actions, but the long term security implications are dire. There will be a time he will regret entrusting key Government positions to inexperienced Jolla folks. One of the reasons why many states are failing in Africa is largely due to ethnic discrimination. Ethnic discrimination is a recipe for civil war.

CHAPTER NINE

A TRIBUTE TO DOT FAAL AND
THE FALLEN NOVEMBER 11 SOLDIERS

I was pretty young when the late Lieutenant Abdoulie Faal, AKA Dot Faal was hosted by my Dad in the early eighties in our house in Touba Murit to head a team of Census clerks in the Niaminas. Dot Faal was either about to graduate from the Armitage High School, or has already graduated.

I can vividly remember my Dad introducing us to Dot. He told us that Mr. Faal was originally from Balangarr, and was in the village to conduct a Census for the then PPP administration.

At the time, Dot was not a soldier. He was a civilian. A very sharp fellow, very intelligent, and friendly. He was some kind of a brother to me. He spends time with the family: eating, chatting, and laughing. I can still reminisce on our old fine days in Niamina.

My Dad had allocated him with a single room, where he stayed until the completion of his assignment. Dot enjoyed his stay in Niamina. He was not treated as a stranger, but a family member. He was told to feel at home.

During the day, Dot will visit "house to house" to gather the number of household residing in a given home before he will retire back to the house in the evening. We brew Attaya together.

He was a calligraphic writer. Occasionally, he will scribble words on the wall, or on a piece of paper as a form of exhibiting his writing skills. We admired his calligraphy.

Occasionally, during his leisure time, he will accompany me to Dankunku to take my Dad's lunch. My Dad is a Taylor by profession. He is widely known in Niamina.

I lost contact with Dot Faal after he left the village. I was made to understand that he later joined the Gambia National Army (GNA) now known as the Gambia Armed Forces.

It was in November of 1994, I learned that he was implicated in a coup, and was murdered by soldiers led by the defunct Junta Vice Chairman Sanna Bairo Sabally, Edward Singhatey, Yankuba Touray and others. Dot Faal was killed alongside with Fafa Nyang, Basiru Barrow, Gibril Saye, Ebrima Ceesay of Kaur, and a host of other soldiers.

After killing the gallant soldiers and officers of the armed forces, Sabally instructed Baboucarr Jatta, the former Army Commander to dump their remains in a mass grave next to the toilets at the Yundum Barracks. It was a sad day in the Gambia. The accused army officers were summarily executed in grand style without form of justice accorded to them to prove their innocence. This was the darkest day in Gambia's coup history.

Some of the murdered soldiers left kids behind—some of whom are today eighteen years old. These kids have no idea as to how their daddies look like. They were pretty young, when Sabally, and his partners in crime gruesomely murdered their parents.

The lucky families were able to migrate to Europe, the United States, and elsewhere around the world in search of save heaven since the junta headed by dictator Jammeh has taken the lives of their loved ones. Mr. Jammeh's eighteen years rule has caused untold suffering and nightmares to oppress Gambians.

Basiru Barrow's daughter is said to be residing in the United States. Gibril Saye had left a child behind; who has has just turned eighteen. These kids have been black listed by President Jammeh. There is no security clearance for them to take up jobs in his administration. The army is a no go area for them. They are being punished because of their murdered parents.

I was made to understand that the late Almamo Manneh named his child after President Jammeh. Almamo's son couldn't witness his Daddy raising him as a child. His fine Mum singlehandedly raised the kids with the help of some family members and loved ones. The boy's Dad Almamo Manneh, a former strong loyalist of President Jammeh was ambushed and killed by Jammeh's thugs. He was accused of coup plot.

Interior Minister Ousman Sonko, aided by other Jammeh confidants framed Almamo Manneh, alongside with Landing Sanneh, a childhood friend of Mr. Jammeh—accusing them of plotting to overthrow the President.

Mr. Manneh was tricked by Sonko, and co to meet with them at a location in the Greater Banjul Area, to "discuss important issues" only for him to be ambushed and killed. He left his wife and kids at home—thinking that he was meeting with sincere comrades—only to be killed upon arrival at the designated appointment location.

Gambians should realize that Yahya Jammeh's eighteen years rule has rendered many families orphanage. He is more than determined today to kill Gambians than ever before. Rise up Gambia and take your country back from this monster.

For Sanna Bairo Sabally, we say, the crimes that you have committed against our people will never go unpunished. You will have your day in court God willing. May the murdered soldiers rest in perfect peace.

CHAPTER TEN

SIGNS OF CIVIL WAR IN THE GAMBIA

Gambia's buffoonery dictator Yahya Jammeh has created the conditions for civil war to take place in The Gambia. Mr. Jammeh's monopoly of the nation's ailing economy, administration of justice, coupled with his flagrant violation of the country's constitution, the basic human rights, and liberties of oppressed Gambians, is a recipe for national disaster. The Gambia is sitting on a timing bomb. It's on the verge of exploding. The country is on the brink of total collapse. The dictator has lost touch with the realities on the ground and is living on a borrowed time. Anything could happen in the Gambian in coming days and months. There is a social breakdown, and its ramifications could be dire.

Gambians across the country be it pro, or anti Jammeh establishment had common concerns today: One, the naked lack of justice in the country, human rights, democracy, and rule of law in this one time stable and prosperous West African nation. Two, Mr. Jammeh's destabilization of the country—with his hateful and tribal speeches against other ethnic groups in The Gambia. Thirdly, the growing culture of corruption in Jammeh's so called "Government" which is not serving the interest of its subjects, but the dictator, and his closest confidants. This regime does not subscribe to democratic tenets, and values. It's a one man rule, in which monster Jammeh divides, and rule the country. Jammeh has destroyed the fabric of society in the Gambia. He has steadily undermined our nation since coming to power through illegal means. His objective is to ruin the Gambia before his imminent fall.

It's imperative to note that there are various factors responsible for civil wars in Africa. For example, Hunger, rising poverty, lack of equitable distribution of a nation's wealth, judicious management of a given country's national resources, institutionalized Government corruption, lawlessness, tribal retribution, discrimination, and lack of Government accountability are some of the causative agents of civil strife on the continent.

And in the case of The Gambia, where dictator Jammeh thinks that he can rule by employing fear tactics to suppress dissent, and the basic rights, and liberties of Gambians, in the form of using some of the renegade members of the country's security forces to arrest, torture, and in some occasions kill their fellow countrymen—just to perpetuate himself into power; it's crucially imperative to note that The Gambia has met the conditions that constitute civil unrest in Africa.

The writings are already on the wall for a civil war in The Gambia. The ordinary man in the streets can smell civil war in The Gambia. Our people, including the Government should cease to live in denial, and admit that the country is in deep, deep trouble. Without justice, fair-play, and responsible Government, peace cannot be guaranteed. Injustices anywhere, is a recipe for disaster. And tyrants like Yahya Jammeh self perpetuate themselves in power by employing the fear rule tactics to tame political opponents.

Gambia you better brace up for the inevitable. The current status quo, under the leadership of Yahya Jammeh is untenable. This regime is not responsive to the plight of Gambians. It's an illegitimate regime bent on undermining freedom! It is not a credible regime that will end the suffering of our people. It's a regime that survives on terror and deception.

To put it mildly: There is no government in The Gambia today. What we have is a one man robbing the state in the name of Governance. Through his office, Yahya Jammeh, has hijacked Gambia's economy just for the sake of sheer greed, and lack of patriotism.

Mr. Jammeh, does not only marginalize the private sector business community here, but he actively competes with them in almost all the sectors of our nation's fragile economy. And yet, this was the guy supposedly voted into office to preside over the affairs of the country. He was never elected into office to meddle into economic income generating ventures. Today, Yahya Jammeh's Gambia's leading business tycoon. He is into all kinds of business ventures. Jammeh doesn't have time to preside over the affairs of the Gambian nation. He is busy pursuing and protecting his business interests within and outside the frontiers of the Gambia.

No one here dares question Jammeh's illegal business activities—not even the opposition. He thinks that he can use his office to perpetrate corruption, crimes against citizens, and the state.

After having openly bragged before National television that "no coup de tat, or elections" can remove him from power, Mr. Jammeh even went as far as extending an invitation to his oppressed citizens to emulate their North African brothers, who successfully toppled some autocratic regimes in Africa—notably in Egypt, Tunisia, and of recent Libya. Mr. Jammeh vows that he will not allow a situation like the Arab Spring to take place in The Gambia, where he maintained a strong grip of the impoverished country. He said he is prepared to cut off the heads of 10,000 Gambians if it means maintaining his despotic regime. We hear you loud, and clear Jammeh!

In a span of eighteen years, Mr. Jammeh has transformed The Gambia as a rogue state. He mystifies himself with all kinds of claims, and bogus academic titles. State radio, and television, devotes 24 hours coverage of Jammeh's activities. It's considered a taboo to feature opposition views, or dissent on the public media. It's all about Jammeh, Jammeh, Jammeh, and his government.

In an attempt to have direct monopoly of the private media, known here as the "independent press" Mr. Jammeh purchased the country's first private daily newspaper, the Daily Observer Company, formally owned by the exiled Liberian journalist Kenneth Y Best. He also uses certain members of the security forces on his "hit squad payroll" to arrest, torture, kill local journalists, and firebomb media houses he perceives as anti Government.

Since the advent of his rule, three journalists have been murdered so far, media houses touched, and journalists forced into exile. The local press practiced self censorship in fear of being arrested, jailed, or a worst case scenario having their newspapers shutdown.

Mr. Jammeh's ultimate objective is to have a Gambia without an independent press. A Gambia, where semi literate journalists will sang his praises, and ignore the crimes he perpetrates on a daily basis against our citizens. A Gambia, in which he can steal, and no journalist dares write about it. A Gambia that can be transformed as a narcotic nation and no law enforcement officer dare investigating its leader. A Gambia, in which he appoints his tribesmen, and empowers them with positions of authority to cover his crimes against humanity. A Gambia, in which Mr. Jammeh uses to pursue his economic dream to the expense of the suffering masses. A Gambia, in which he can use Nigerian mercenary magistrates, and judges to falsely imprison its citizens. A Gambia, in which he can turn families against each other. A Gambia, in which lies, and deception rule. A Gambia, in which there is no justice. A Gambia, in which the poor is exploited by the President. A Gambia, in which judges, and state lawyers turn as puppets for the dictator. A Gambia, in which he can force its citizens to work on his Kanilai farm without any form of compensation. A Gambia, in which he can transform as a police state.

Little, did our ignoramus "President" realize that when citizen's basic freedoms and liberties are under attack, they resort to any measures to reclaim their rights. And sooner, or later, there will be a popular revolution in The Gambia. The writings are already on the wall for Jammeh's imminent fall.

Change will come as a surprise to the dictator, and his followers. There are many forces working on salvaging the nation from Jammeh's misrule. But our concern is the lack of coordination among these forces—who all had singular objective—that's to liberate the oppressed Gambian masses. There are what we called the "known, and the unknown" forces. These pro democracy forces are steadily working towards accomplishing the mission. But without unity, sense of purpose, and direction, there will hardly be any meaningful change that the country and her people are yearning for. Gambians should be united and recognize that Jammeh's regime is not the promised regime. This regime represents failure. It represents underdevelopment.

We hope Gambians will effect the change that they desire. But for heaven sake, do not allow the efforts that you worked for so hard in recent months to degenerate into a civil war! Be professional, and continue to serve as Ambassadors of your own destiny.

Together, Gambians can spearhead the long anticipated change without allowing blood thirsty dictator Jammeh to further destabilize the nation. This is a challenge for all Gambians. The common enemy is Yahya Jammeh. Let us save this country from the looming civil war, which is about to upset the nation's much cherished peace. The army, the police, and the NIA are of no exception in this patriotic call. Let us save The Gambia from a civil war!

CHPATER ELEVEN

GAMBIA IS A DRUG HUB NATION

The Gambia has been transformed as a drug hub nation. South American drug cartels are using the country, as a transit point to traffic drugs to Western nations. Over one billion dollars street value of cocaine was intercepted in the heart of the Gambia two years ago. The traffickers obtained license from the Government to invest into the country's fishing industry—only for them to exploit the corrupt leadership of President Yahya Jammeh by allegedly buying them out to traffic drugs into the Gambia. Tons of cocaine is hidden in that impoverished country.

The regime, under the leadership of dictator Yahya Jammeh is not making any serious efforts in combating narcotic trafficking in the region. Imagine the President annexing the anti narcotic unit under his office; had his brother Benedict Jammeh to head the institution together with his other tribesmen. He made the decision after the seizure of the one billion dollars worth of cocaine in the Gambia. How do you expect justice Gambia, when the President is seen to be meddling into the administration of justice in this country? Jammeh wants to be a narcotic officer at the same time running the affairs of the nation. His fingerprints are all over the place.

Gambia's drug trade is a complex one. There are public officials allegedly on the payroll of drug cartels. The traffickers allegedly had the backing of the Jammeh administration. There is no way that such a high volume of cocaine can be trafficked into the Gambia without the regime knowing about it. The drug trade is an inside job. There is a powerful force within Banjul protecting the traffickers.

The former police chief Essa Badjie has made numerous remarks in court suggesting that the President's name was allegedly being associated with cocaine trafficking. Mr. Badjie was tasked to investigate those accusing the President of drug trade—only for Badjie to be slammed with life imprisonment after been found guilty of economic crime and other corruption related charges.

Interestingly, after the seizure of the tons of cocaine from the South American nationals, dictator Jammeh ordered for the seizure of the drug cartels offices situated in Kanifing. He also allegedly pocketed the millions of dollars caught with the accused persons. There were no monetary exhibits tendered in court, when the accused persons were convicted. And it was reported by the state controlled media GRTS after the arrest of the accused persons that the arresting team recovered several thousands of Euros and fire arms from the drug dealers. There was no such evidence in court tendered. The recovered cocaine money and the fire arms have disappeared in the thin air.

The judge who presided over the case passed his judgment without asking the prosecution to produce the confiscated money. We also haven't heard about the destruction of the tons of cocaine that was seized in the Gambia. Mr. Ben Jammeh told a colleague that the state is waiting for the United Nations and other security allies around the world to witness the drug destruction. At the same time, drugs are reported missing on a daily basis at NDEA drug store. We also heard about NDEA agents supplying seized drugs to local drug dealers to help market the drugs for them.

Mr. Jammeh did not stop at that. He also transformed the seized Holligam offices formerly leased by the South American so called investors as the new National Drug Enforcement Agency District office in the KMC area. What does this tells you Gambia? It means a rotten system is occupying an office which used to be occupied by drug cartels. How can Jammeh reconcile his actions, when he can occupy a building belonging to a private Gambian citizen without legal sanctioning? Yet, he claimed to be trying to make the Gambia a "drug free" nation. How can Jammeh convince us that he is not affiliated with the jailed South American nationals?

Mr. Jammeh surrounding himself with his biological family members and ethnic group to help him combat the country's drug menace raises a red flag to the average observer. If Jammeh is truly committed to fighting drugs, he should allow the police, NDEA and the NIA to operate independently without his Government's interference. Any attempt on the side of Jammeh to control these security institutions will send a wrong message to the outside world.

Where on earth, does a President oversees the administration of a country's anti narcotic unit? It's only in the Gambia that such a thing can happen. There is no separation of power, checks and balances in the Gambia. One man called Yahya Jammeh is deciding the fate of a population of about 1.6 million people—less than the size of Delaware. If Jammeh is allegedly into drug trafficking, there is no credible law enforcement agency in the Gambia that can investigate him. Mr. Jammeh dictates the operational activities of the NDEA. He has total control of all the security agencies in the country. His brother Ben Jammeh takes orders from him.

It's also imperative to note that the Interior Minister Ousman Sonko came from the same ethnic background with President Jammeh. Mr. Sonko pledges his loyalty to Jammeh and not the Gambian nation. How can such a man of questionable character stick to his oath of office if Mr. Jammeh can manipulate him, and make him do things against his own conscience? It is not possible. This is the guy coordinating Jammeh's alleged terror machine in Banjul. His hands are allegedly stained with blood. He is notorious to be an alleged career killer.

It's also worth noting that the head of the National Intelligence Agency is a Jolla. Numo Kujabi is working for dictator Jammeh's interest. There is no doubt about that. Numo will never go against Jammeh's interest—given their ethnic ties.

The Gambian Ports Authority too is also controlled by Jammeh's tribesmen. Momodou Lamin Gibba is the Managing Director of the Gambia Ports Authority. Mr. Gibba's Dad Babai Gibba of Dobong raised Yahya Jammeh, when he was going to school in Bwiam. ML Gibba and Jammeh are kind of brothers. He too will never work against Jammeh's interest. He will not stop the dictator and his cohorts from using the ports as an avenue to carry out their alleged illicit business activities.

Half of the time the Jammeh's containers are never inspected at the ports on arrival. Mr. Jammeh can import anything into the country without anyone questioning him. He enjoys free pass at the ports. His containers are escorted in and out of the ports uninspected. No one dares inspect Jammeh's containers.

Given the underlining factors highlighted above, it would be very difficult for the Gambia to emerge as a drug free nation. The Gambia needs viable, professional, and strong security institutions free of government interference, or monopoly to be able to effectively combat narcotic trafficking. The Gambia, as a nation, cannot afford to have a President, who is in the business of welcoming drug cartels into the country in the name of investment, only for him turn around to police the state. There should be checks and balances in government, if this country truly wants to be categorized as a serious nation complementing global efforts to eradicate drug trafficking.

Beside, the drug menace challenges facing the country, the Gambia has been linked to harboring Hezbollah financers. Lebanese businesses are using the country as a save heaven to raise funds in the name of investment.

The country's President Yahya Jammeh too, was allegedly busted with an arms shipment from Iran, destined for his Kanilai farm. Thirteen containers filled with deadly weapons belonging to President Jammeh were confiscated in Nigeria by Custom agents. The secret arms shipment between Iran and The Gambia has been going on for three years, according to competent sources. An administration official in Banjul said the intercepted arms were meant for homeland security in the wake of the arms scandal, but sources indicated that Jammeh is an alleged career arms merchant, who had made couple of millions of dollars from the illicit trade. Some of the Iranian arms have landed in the arms of rebels in the Southern province of Casamance and in the Middle East.

CHAPTER TWELVE

GAMBIA'S VICE PRESIDENT ON JOURNALIST DEYDA HYDARA'S MURDER

Gambia's Vice President Isatou Njie said she met with Senegalese President Macky Sall during the United Nations Summit, who assured her that there was no problem between Senegal and the Gambia, even though the two Senegalese death row inmates were executed by the Gambia government. She informed me that during her meeting with President Macky Sall, the Senegalese President delegated her to convey a message of goodwill and brotherly greetings to his counterpart President Yahya Jammeh after Macky had assured her that there was no problem between Senegal and the Gambia. She claimed that Macky had also told her that the execution of Ms. Tabara Samba and Gibbi Bah was in line with Gambia's laws and Senegal had no problem with her neighbor's actions.

Freedom Newspaper Managing Editor Pa Nderry M'Bai spoke with the country's Vice President Isatou Njie Saidy, who was in New York to attend the United Nations Summit. The Vice President was contacted at her hotel room in Yonkers to comment on a wide range of issues: the execution of the country's nine death row inmates by the President Yahya Jammeh, the aftermath of the inmates killing, the situation of Gambia's relationship with its neighbor Senegal after the execution of the two Senegalese inmates, the demise of journalist Chief Ebrima Manneh while in state custody, the massacre of the April 10 student rioters, and the murder of Deyda Hydara.

Known for his investigative skills, Mr. M'Bai posed as a strong supporter of the President's ruling APRC Party, when he called the Vice President in the morning of September 27. A hotel phone operator transferred the line after Mr. M'Bai requested to speak with Gambia's Vice President Isatou Njie Saidy. No questions were asked as to who was on the line. No screening!

I had called the previous night and was told that there was no one in the Vice President's hotel room. The hotel phone operator put me on hold for about ten minutes, while he repeatedly tried to transfer the call to the Vice President's room, but he came back and told me that she was not available. "Sir, sorry there is no one in the room," the hotel phone operator told me. I said to him I have to call back later. I continued working on my upcoming book.

I called back the next day Thursday, and I was lucky to get hold of the Vice President on the phone. The Vice President was very receptive, when I introduced myself to her as a party supporter. I was surprised that she talked to me freely without even asking for my name. She only wanted to know whether I live in New York, and I responded in the affirmative. She was satisfied with my introduction that I was a member of their ruling party. She briefly spoke to me in the local Mandinka dialect after I told her that my Mandinka was that good. She then asked for my ethnic group, and I responded by telling her that I am a wollof. She told me that she was fluent in wollof, and we could proceed with the conversation.

Initially, I had wanted to fake my voice, but once I realize that the unsuspecting Vice President never doubted my claim of being a party supporter, I spoke to her freely. She appeared very happy to receive my phone call. I began the conversation by thanking the Vice President, and the President Yahya Jammeh for their able leadership in steering the affairs of the Gambian nation. I told her that I was her strong supporter, including President Jammeh, and it was great to touch base with her. The Vice President was convinced by my statement" pledging my loyalty to the President and his ruling APRC party.

We briefly exchanged greetings before I raised the issue of the execution of the nine death row inmates. I spoke about my opposition to the regime's move to take the lives of the inmates. The Vice President assured me that the President had halted the executions for now. She said the President was just trying to set an example so that would be criminals will draw lessons from the executions. She said the move followed a visit made to her office by some concerned Gambian Council of elders, who prevailed on the President to spare the lives of the remaining inmates.

The President has agreed to impose a moratorium on the executions, she said. She told me that Jammeh killed none security and political detainees. The move behind the President's actions she said was to fight crimes. She said there is a rising crime rate in the Gambia, and that the President thought that the best way to mitigate the problem was to set a drastic example on inmates who were condemned to death for murder.

The Vice President said Mr. Jammeh never targeted political prisoners during the executions. She said if Jammeh had taken such a move the world would have a different perception of his regime. "Thank God that no political prisoner or security detainee was killed," she said.

She maintains that the executions were legally justified and that let me not be swayed by critics of the President in the diaspora such as Pa Nderry M'Bai, and Essa Bokarr Sey, Gambia's former Ambassador to Washington DC. The Vice President repeatedly complained about Mr. M'Bai and Mr. Sey branding them as enemies of the Gambia.

She even claimed that President Jammeh sponsored Mr. M'Bai's mother to attend pilgrimage in Mecca. She also accuses Ambassador Sey of embezzling Government funds while serving as a Diplomat in the United States. Mr. Sey has repeatedly denied such allegations. He said he is willing to submit himself before any credible Government inquiry post Jammeh era to prove his innocence.

The Vice President rained all kinds of personal attacks against Mr. M'Bai and Sey. She told me that Editor M'Bai neglected his parents and is using the Internet as an outlet to smear the image of President Jammeh and his Government. She said Gambians should not listen to M'Bai because his agenda is to get fame, sell his newspaper, and undermine the current administration with his hateful writings against the status quo.

The Vice President at some point of my conversation with her, she branded me as an 'illegitimate son" who has nothing to offer to his country—besides giving a wrong perception about the President and the country. She said only fools will listen to Mr. M'Bai and Essa Sey. She said she doesn't read junk news, and propaganda.

The Vice President said she is a distance relative of Ambassador Sey. Although she shuns Essa because she thought that the direction the former Ambassador is taking is the wrong way. She said Essa ought to have returned back home in the Gambia, when he was recalled by the President to face an inquiry, but she said the former Ambassador refused, and decided to stay in the United States to apply for asylum. She said Essa has nothing to tell President Jammeh because he refuses to return home to clear his image.

Essa, she said, walked his way through the top by getting closer to influential relatives in the Government, including the Kujabi brothers to secure white color job in Jammeh's regime. She knew Mr. Sey as a retired soldier, only for Sey to be appointed by the President years later as an Ambassador to the US, Taiwan, and France.

The Vice President said she doesn't read Mr. Sey's attacks directed at her on the Internet, but occasionally she sometimes received briefings from some friends and relatives who informed her about some of Sey's critical postings against her person.

"I don't read the junk on the Internet. Essa Sey, and Pa Nderry M'Bai are loose cannons. They don't spare anyone. They attack the President and everyone in his Government," she said.

At some point of our conversation, I began to wonder whether the Vice President was really security conscious, and Presidential—given her outspoken nature without weighing the implications of some of her statements. Some of the issues she mentioned during the conversation should not have been communicated to an unknown caller posing as a party supporter. She went too far by disclosing state matters that she ought to have kept to herself.

For example, she talked about meeting President Macky Sall of Senegal, and the issues she discussed with Sall about the execution of Tabara Samba and Gibbi Bah, both Senegalese nationals by the Jammeh administration. She also informed me that President Sall had delegated her to convey a message of goodwill and brotherly greetings to his counterpart President Jammeh after Macky had assured her that there was no problem between Senegal and the Gambia. She claimed that Macky had told her that the execution of Tabara Samba and Gibbi Bah was in line with Gambia's laws and Senegal had no problem with Gambia's actions.

The Vice President tried to impress me throughout the conversation by making positive remarks about President Jammeh and the Gambia as a nation. She said President Macky Sall had a fruitful discussion with her, and she was supposed to convey President Sall's message to Jammeh.

The Vice President blamed the likes of Pa Nderry M'Bai and Essa Sey of blowing things out of proportion. She said the online media is bent on giving a bad impression about the Gambia to Senegal. She said the problem with Gambians is lack of patriotism.

"The Senegalese are no fools. They know the realities on the ground. I met President Macky Sall yesterday in New York and he assured me that the relationship between the Gambia and Senegal is growing from strength to strength. There is a cordial bilateral ties between Senegal and the Gambia. It is the media that is blowing things out of proportion," she posited.

In a half an hour phone conversation, the Vice President also discusses about the massacre of the fourteen unarmed Gambian students back in April 2000. She used the phone conversation to throw dictator

Jammeh and his cohorts under the bus. She cleared herself from any wrongdoing.

The Vice President said she acted based on security briefings she received from the relevant security heads by announcing on state media on the day of the incident that the students killed themselves. She said she was not on the ground to witness the student riots.

"I reported about what I was told that the shooting originates from the student protesters. I was not there to know what actually transpired. You know that . . . I was in my office waiting to meet with the students so that we can resolve the matter. I was briefed that the students started the shooting and in the process some lives were lost," she said.

The Vice President did not rule out that there were some bad guys within the crowd to cause trouble. She said some opposition elements might have joined the students to shoot at the police.

On the issue of journalist Deyda Hydara's murder, Ms. Njie Saidy said it's up to the Gambian people to judge about what Editor M'Bai had reported in the past about the President's involvement into the murder of Hydara. She confirmed that shortly after the murder of Hydara, President Jammeh sent a delegation to the journalist's family to express his condolence. She said the late Deyda Hydara was a close friend of her late husband Jaye Saidy. Mr. Jaye Saidy works as an Associate Editor at the Point Newspaper prior to his demise. This author worked with Mr. Saidy at the Point. He was a perfect gentleman.

The Vice President also talked about the demise of journalist Ebrima Chief Manneh. She said she doesn't know Chief Manneh in person, but stated that the journalist might as well die while trying to migrate to Europe. She said many Gambian youths died on their way to the Canary Island. She said it's wrong for anyone to blame the Government for Chief Manneh's death after she was told that Chief was arrested by Gambia's security agents by this author.

At the end of our conversation, Editor M'Bai formally identified himself to the Vice President. The Vice President later downplayed the entire conversation by claiming that she knew that it was Mr. M'Bai calling.

"Pa Nderry, I knew that it was you calling. You guys are fond of calling and recording people. I am speaking my mind. I have nothing to hide. Even if you had indentified yourself I would have spoken to you. I am not that type of person. I am not a Vice President for the APRC, but for the Gambia. I treat all Gambians equally. After all, you are a Gambian," she said.

The Vice President later toned down her language. She appealed to me to "be fair and balance" with the President since he is hospitable to my parents. She said President Jammeh supports people he even doesn't know. She wanted Mr. Mr. M'Bai to be bit considerate with President Jammeh in his writings. I reminded her that my parent's political opinion doesn't concern me. That my parents are free to affiliate themselves with any political party of their choice.

Earlier on, Editor M'Bai asked Ms. Njie Saidy about any possible investment opportunities in the Gambia. The Vice President said the Gambia is a safe place for investment. I reminded her about the economic backlash that might follow after the execution of the inmates—stressing to her that tourists and investors might be afraid to visit the Gambia due to the incident. She assured me that there is no need for panic. She claimed that Gambia's tourism sector is booming, and that Tourism Minister Fatou Mass Jobe was scheduled to meet with delegates at the UN conference on Thursday afternoon to brief them about investment prospects in the Gambia. She even wanted to link me up with Tourism Minister Fatou Mass Jobe so that she can brief me about the situation of the tourism sector in the Gambia.

I also raised the case of the Touray brothers of the Pristine company with the Vice President. After informing her about the mistreatment Abdouraman Touray and his brother Assan Touray suffered in the hands of Jammeh's regime, following contractual dispute between the two brothers and the Government, the Vice President said the matter has been amicably settled. She said the Touray brothers have since apologized to the regime, and that their case had been dropped. She said the issue, which warranted the contractual dispute had to do with biometric identity card the Touray brothers reached with the Jammeh Government. She informed me that she met the CEO of the company Abdouraman Touray in the past. She said Mr. Touray is a relative of politician Assan Musa Camara.

Highly placed sources familiar with the Touray brothers case disagree with the Vice President's assertions. The Vice President, said our source has not been properly informed about the developments. "It was the government that apologized through the Solicitor General to the company and promised to pay Pristine the money owed to the company. As to date however, the government has still not yet fulfilled its contractual obligations, "our source stated, while strongly rejecting the VP'S claims that the Touray brothers apologized to the state.

"There was no such apology made to the state as claimed by Isatou Njie Saidy. It was the state who in fact apologized to the Touray brothers for the matter to be settled out of court."

Continuing her grand testimony about her in-depth knowledge about the Gambia, and the President Yahya Jammeh, Isatou Njie also commented on her boss's matrimonial life. She denied news reports suggesting that President Jammeh recently married a Ghanaian girl. The Vice President told me in a phone conversation that she was only aware of one lady married to President Jammeh, in the person of Zeinab Souma Jammeh, a Moroccan national. The Vice President strongly debunked such reports, while blaming Gambian hate mongers for being responsible for the spread of the rumor.

When I raised the issue of Alima Sallah, the daughter of OG Sallah, Gambia's Ambassador to the Kingdom of Saudi Arabia, who was married to President Jammeh few years ago, the Vice President said she was not sure whether Madam Sallah was still married to the President. Although, she confirmed Alima Sallah married to Jammeh about three years ago. She appeared to have downplayed Alima's marital relationship with Jammeh. It took her few seconds before she could answer to my question.

"That was the only recent marital relationship between the President, and Alima Sallah that I am aware of. It is false for anyone to suggest that President Jammeh recently married to a Ghanaian lady. He is not married to any Ghanaian lady," the Vice President stated.

Madam Isatou Njie Saidy also talked about President Jammeh's failure to attend the United Nations Summit. She said the President is on vacation and is busy working at his farm in Kanilai. She said she has been representing the Gambian leader on numerous occasions at the UN Summit.

"The President doesn't have time for these useless Gambians protesting at the UN. You will be surprised to learn that these protesters do not even get close to the UN. The security wouldn't allow them to get close to us," she said whiling renewing her attacks at Ambassador Sey and journalist Pa Nderry M'Bai.

The Vice President said Mr. Sey's relatives, such as Alpha Khan, and Omar Khan are working for President Jammeh. She told me that Mr. Sey will not heed to family advice to stop attacking her on the Internet. Ms. Njie Saidy said she is preoccupied on her work as the country's Vice President. She will not waste her precious time responding to Mr. Sey, or Pa Nderry M'Bai. She appealed to Gambians not to listen Essa Sey and Pa Nderry M'Bai. The two, she said, are looking for cheap fame, and also to destroy the image of the President, and everyone working for Jammeh.

The Vice President also claimed that Editor M'Bai has no place in post Jammeh era. She said Mr. M'Bai is not fit to work for any future Government in the Gambia. She used my conversation with her to appeal to her countrymen to please ignore M'Bai and Sey for the sake of national development. She said both Sey and M'Bai will never return to the Gambia—given their open hatred for the country, and the present Government. She said a true patriot will not be hostile to his country. But in the case of M'Bai and Sey they have openly demonstrated their hatred for the Gambia and President Jammeh, she told me. She said President Jammeh made Essa Sey an Ambassador, but the latter has proven to be ungrateful to the Gambian leader.

"Do not be surprised if they turn against the Gambia and start supporting Senegal. These are bad citizens, who do not have the country's interest at heart. All their actions is geared towards plunging the SeneGambian region into turmoil. But Senegal will never allow that to happen. I met President Macky Sall, and he has confided to me in private that no one can separate the two nations. We discussed about the execution of their nationals by the Gambian Government. Sall assured me that Senegal has not taken offense of what we have done. Let Pa Nderry and Essa Sey keep talking. Even in Senegal the death penalty is enforced. People are killed in Senegal," the Vice President claimed.

Regarding the growing online opposition in the diaspora, the Vice President said Gambians back home do not listen to Pa Nderry and Essa Sey. She said the Internet cannot make the opposition to win an election. She told me that Gambians are in full support of the President—adding that Sey and M'Bai are on a waste venture. The only people who listen to Essa and Pa Nderry are the enemies of the Gambia, she said. These are ignorant Gambians, who do not have any clue about what is happening in the Gambia, Ms. Njie Saidy added.

Commenting on her political opinion, the Vice President said she is not in the business of dirty politics. She said she treats all Gambians with respect. "This is a small country. We are all interrelated. You will be surprised to learn that I am related to one of the wives of the opposition leader Ousainou Darboe. I am related to Darboe by virtue of my sister marrying to him. If I use my position to insult Darboe, then it means I am insulting myself. Be it Pa Nderry M'Bai, Essa Sey, or any other Gambian in the opposition, we are all related. That is why you will never hear me castigating the opposition. That's not part of my political chemistry," she said.

The Vice President said Mr. M'Bai and Sey should learn to treat people with respect. The two, she went on, spare no one in Jammeh's regime. "Don't you hear them saying that President Jammeh is a non Gambian? If they brand me a citizen of Kollack Senegal, it is not something new. They said Yahya Jammeh is not a Gambian. I am sure you heard them saying this," she said.

Going by Isatou Njie's voluntary statement, it is apparent that the Jammeh regime survives on gossip. The Vice President spent about half an hour gossiping about Pa Nderry M'Bai and Essa Sey. She thought that she was communicating with a sincere, loyal and genuine party supporter. Who knows how many APRC supporters Isatou briefed about the President's activities, state secrets, and other issues concerning the diasporan Gambian community? Only God knows.

The Vice President has not demonstrated good leadership during her conversation with Mr. M'Bai. She has done more harm than good. She runs her mouth throughout the program. It was like a comedy to many Freedom radio listeners. How on earth can a country's Vice President behave in such a manner? She was completely pinned down by the Freedom Editor.

Gambians are now beginning to believe that the likes of Isatou Njie Saidy and Yahya Jammeh are the ones leaking the secrets of the administration to the world. Isatou is very vulnerable. She talks freely without weighing the implications of her actions. Jammeh is a photocopy of Isatou Njie. He is worst than Isatou when it comes to running his mouth.

Another thing Gambians can learn from Isatou Njie Saidy's revelations, it tells the average reader about the quality of leadership we have in the Gambia. If you have maroons like Yahya Jammeh and Isatou Njie Saidy heading the country, what else do you expect? The regime in Banjul is a disservice to our country, and her people.

Gambia's Vice President Isatou Njie Saidy has said that President Macky Sall of Senegal merely condemned the execution of its nationals by the Gambian Government just for the sake of calming down raging Senegalese citizens in the wake of the secret executions, but in reality, the Vice President said Sall has no problem with the Gambia executing its constitutional mandate by killing Senegalese death row inmates. The Vice President also said based on the feedbacks she received from President Sall during private talks she had with the Senegalese leader at the United Nations conference in New York; she was told by Sall that Senegal has no problem with the Gambia enforcing the death penalty.

She claimed that Macky told her that the Gambia acted in accordance with its laws and that no amount of propaganda can separate the two nations.

The Gambian Vice President, who was taken off guard by the Freedom Newspaper Editor, posing as a strong supporter of the President and his ruling party, spoke eloquently on matters relating to Gambia's foreign policy, Sub-Regional issues, the President's marital life, and the country's domestic politics.

The Vice President said the reaction taken by President Sall in condemning the execution of Ms. Tabara Samba, and Gibbi Bah, both Senegalese death row inmates in the Gambia, was highly anticipated—given the domestic pressure President Sall has to endure in the aftermath of the killing of two of their nationals by the regime in Banjul.

The Vice President argued throughout my conversation with her about the justification of the executions. She even tried to compare President Obama's reaction to the assassination of the United States Ambassador to Libya Christopher Stevens with the reaction made by Obama's counterpart Senegalese President Macky Sall in regards to the execution of the death row inmates in the Gambia.

"You remember when the US Ambassador to Libya got killed, and President Barack Obama made a reaction similar to that of President Macky Sall's condemnation of Gambia's execution of the death row inmates. Such reactions are expected. In order for President Obama to calm down Americans in the wake of the assassination of their Ambassador to Libya, he has to step-up to the plate by condemning the incident just for the sake of downplaying the mounting political tensions within America. Obama spoke just for the sake of calming down the situation in America. That's part of politics. President Macky Sall too did the same thing. Sall condemned the Gambia executions just for the sake of appeasing aggrieved Senegalese. He never meant his words. That I can tell you. I had a meeting with President Sall and he told me unequivocally that The Gambia is on its own right to enforce the death penalty. Sall has also informed me that his Government has no problem with the executions," said Vice President y Njie Saidy.

"Do not listen to what our detractors are saying. It's the people talking; trying to blow things out of proportion. There is no problem between Senegal and the Gambia. That I can assure you. If Macky had not condemned the executions, his opponents would have politicized it. What else do you expect from Macky? He has to do what he has done to win the confidence of the Senegalese people. Between the two countries, we know what's happening. Let them say whatever they want to say. The leadership of the two nations are talking. There is no problem," she said.

Ms. Njie Saidy said one of the reasons why the Senegalese Government was angry with the Gambian High Commissioner assigned to Dakar was due to his lack of timely response to an invitation that was extended to the High Commissioner by the Senegalese President Macky Sall for him to meet with him to discuss the Banjul death row executions.

"The Secretary created the confusion He hid the letter that was addressed to the High Commissioner and was from the Senegalese Government. The problem has been taken care of now," she said.

The Vice President's comparison of President Obama's reaction to the killing of the US Ambassador to Libya and that of Macky Sall's remarks in regards to the Gambian executions, clearly exposes Isatou Njie Saidy's lack of empathy and her diplomatic ignorance when it comes to global issues. Her remarks also suggest that she could be a potential terrorist supporter, or sympathizer. Any right minded human being should sympathize with America about the terror assault directed at their Embassy in Libya. But the Gambian Vice President has decided to use the Libyan terror attack to defame the American President, and also to deceive and mislead this caller. How on earth can Isatou Njie Saidy recklessly politicize the killing of an American diplomat, when peace loving countries are working with the United States Government to combat global terrorism? Her conduct is just insane!

I do not see the connections between the Libyan terror attack and the Gambian death row executions. Unless Isatou Njie Saidy wants to tell us that her boss dictator Yahya Jammeh is a terrorist. If she does said so, she is partly right because Jammeh represents evil. All these years, he has been perpetrating terror on our people.

Gambia's naive Madam Vice President thinks that Obama's condemnation of the Ambassador's murder was politically motivated. She even falsely claimed that the US President's statement was motivated by public pressure to issue such denunciation of the terror attack. She tried to convince me that Obama's reaction was largely shaped by public opinion in America. What a wishful thinking Gambia.

Meanwhile, an unpredictable reception awaits Vice President Isatou Njie Saidy upon her return to Banjul. The dictator is reported to have threatened to confront Madam Njie Saidy upon her return on some of the issues she mentioned during her phone conversation with Editor Pa Nderry M'Bai.

Mr. Jammeh is ragging that the VP commented on his private marital life. This angered him a lot. Mr. Jammeh wants to know from Isatou Njie Saidy, who gave her the permission to brief a foreign journalist about his matrimonial home. The VP has been panicking since the broadcast of her private conversation with Editor M'Bai. She is worried that the dictator might let her go. A worst case scenario, she could be arrested and charged for divulging state secrets to an American journalist.

She was sick for the entire day after my conversation with her. Delegation members tried to console her. She was worried about the remarks she made over the phone. A delegation member tried to downplay the scandal by assuring her that she hasn't done anything wrong.

Isatou Njie Saidy is also the Chairperson of Gambia's National Security Council. All security briefings concerning national security passes through her. Her recent move to openly discuss state related matters with an unknown caller is troubling so to speak. This clearly suggests that the Vice President is not security conscious.

Weeks after my undercover interview with Gambia's Vice President Isatou Njie Saidy, who portrayed the Jammeh dictatorship in the negative light—amid damning revelations about the country's national security secrets, my parents were interviewed by security agents acting under the directives of dictator Yahya Jammeh. Four men showed up at our family home in Touba Murit, in Niamina Dankunku District to conduct a video interview with my family. The delegation also took some photographs of my family including our home.

My Dad is almost ninety years old. The majority of his age mates in the village have died. He has persistently pleaded with me to stop writing about President Jammeh and his government. Left with my parents alone, I should mind my business and focus on other issues outside Gambian politics. But I let them understand that I owe it to my country and her people by serving as a mouthpiece for the oppressed and the voiceless. I also assured them that I harbored no grudges against President Jammeh and his Government. I am merely doing my required journalistic job. Period.

The whole idea behind the interview Jammeh's security agents had with my parents: was to build up a case that President Jammeh took my Mum to Mecca for pilgrimage. Good luck on your cheap propaganda. But what the regime fails to explain to Gambians is that the Saudi government usually allocates free air tickets to poor countries such as the Gambia to enable Muslims to attend pilgrimage in Mecca. The dictator unfortunately is politicizing the Saudi government gift extended to our country. They also wanted to showcase that my parents are in full support of Jammeh and his government. The regime also wanted to portray me as someone who had neglected his parents.

I am on recorded for having said that any day President Jammeh provide proofs that he paid for my Mum's Hajj ticket, I will refund him his money. Jammeh can keep his money. I have been supporting my parents and I do not owe any obligation to Jammeh and his APRC to discuss any financial support that I legitimately provide to my parents. I have my parents blessing. They are happy with me. That is all I needed as a patriotic son of the Gambia.

I have no qualms with my parents supporting the political party of their choice. It is their constitutional right to decide which political leader they wanted to support. I must hasten to add that I will not advise them, or any other Gambian to support President Jammeh and his party. My reasons are well premised.

In my view, President Jammeh and his ruling APRC are not representing the interest of Gambians. Jammeh is not developing the Gambia. He is instead using the office of the President to enrich himself to the expense of the suffering nation. There is also a growing culture of corruption under Jammeh's rule. There is no human rights. There is no free press in the Gambia. Jammeh's regime is dead. All the necessary pillars that should render a government functional had collapsed.

The Jammeh delegation also claimed that they thought that I was from the capital city Banjul. My parents informed them that I was born and raised in Touba Murit. They left and promised to get in touch with them later. The tape was supposed to be handed to President Jammeh. I was also informed that the regime might use the tape for propaganda purposes by airing it on GRTS to discredit me.

Prior to the police in Bassang, and the NIA paying a visit to my parents in Niamina, I was briefed by a member of the NIA that the President has created a special unit to monitor my family and sources suspected of supplying me information from the Gambia.

Initially, I down played the information. But barely one month down the line, I received credible reports that a delegation claiming to be Jammeh's emissary visited my village to interview my parents. The delegation was hosted by one Njie Nget, who happens to be the APRC youth leader in the village. Matter of fact, Mr. Nget is my cousin. Mr. Nget took them to my family home, where the delegation claimed that they were assigned to talk to my parents.

The NIA interview took barely an hour. My parents were asked to state the number of kids they got; children's names, and place of residence within and outside the frontiers of the Gambia. It was an interesting interview.

When my name came up as one of the sons of my Dad, one of the delegation members remarked: "Oh you are Pa Nderry M'Bai's father? We thought that Pa Nderry M'Bai was from Banjul. On the whole, he is from Touba Murit," the delegation member remarked. My Dad in response said: "Yes, Pa Nderry is my son. He is my first son. He was born and raised in Touba Murit."

My Dad, was also asked if he was in touch with me. He informed the delegation that it has been a while that we haven't communicated. He also couldn't tell the delegation where in overseas that I was residing. He informed the delegation that to the best of his recollection, he only knew that I left the country for overseas. He also told them that he doesn't want to speculate about my whereabouts because it has been a while that we have not been in touch.

When I contacted my parents to shed light on their encounter with the government, they were not keen at discussing the matter. They instead advised me to stop criticizing President Jammeh and his government. My Dad told me that he was getting old and I should consider their plight for God sake and refrain from commenting on Gambia related political issues. My parents spoke positively about President Jammeh and his leadership.

I made it categorically clear to them that the political opinion I held against the Jammeh leadership is based on principles. That I do not hate President Jammeh as a person, but I despised the way and manner he presides over the affairs of the nation. I also told them that I value their advice, but it's rather unfortunate that I had to go against their counseling to turn my back against the struggle just for the sake of not offending the status quo in Banjul.

I was also told by a top administration official in Banjul that the President has declared me as his sworn enemy. The official said Jammeh is so desperate about the amount of information reported on the Freedom Newspaper and Freedom Radio about his corrupt practices and some of the crimes being associated with him. The official also told me that the President has on numerous occasions engaged the services of "top marabouts" in the region to help him take my life spiritually, but none of the spiritual assignments have worked so far. He said Jammeh is increasingly worried by the growing support and followers that I am attracting within and outside the country.

"The President thinks that you are out to destroy him and his government. He is telling us that your paper is causing this country to lose millions of dollars worth of foreign aid money. Anyone associated with you has been blacklisted by his government. Your news reportage has caused a devastating blow on the President and his government," the official said.

The official also informed me that Mr. Lamin Nyabally, a Permanent Secretary at the Vice President's office is worried that he might lose his job due to my recent interview with the Vice President. Mr. Nyabally hailed from Niamina Dankunku. He was said to be part of the delegation who accompanied the Vice President to the United Nations Summit in New York. The Vice President and her delegation had a rough time upon their return to Banjul, I was told.

During the weekend, Mr. Njie Nget was contacted by the Jammeh agents to help them locate my junior brother Abdoulie Mbye, who was at the time at my house in Manjie-Kunda. Mr. Mbye had to travel to the village to meet with a television crew said to be from the GRTS. The crew said the initial recording shot by the Jammeh emissaries was not very clear and they wanted to rerecord my parents.

I gathered from reliable sources that my parents were confronted with questions about their son Pa Nderry M'Bai and his Freedom Newspaper. The television crew wanted to know whether my parents were aware of the potential harm Mr. M'Bai and the Freedom Newspaper is causing the country and the government of the day. They also wanted to know if Mr. M'Bai was supportive of his parents financially. My parents support for President Jammeh and his ruling APRC also dominated the interview.

If all worked out well, the Jammeh leadership intends to air the interview on GRTS on Tabaski day. The Jammeh propaganda machine thought that the interview they had with my parents is their biggest scoop of the year. They want to use my name for political gains. But Gambians are no fools to buy their cheap propaganda.

One Sankung Jobarteh, said to be an agent of the NIA, alias Balla Jobarteh, Mr. Tunkara, and Badjie were among the team who visited my family home. The men were polite during their encounter with the Mbye family, I was told. They said they were agents of the regime.

Just for the record: I want to inform the world that a close associate of President Jammeh, a prominent Lebanese businessman, has hired a North Carolina Private Investigative Firm to monitor my movements within Raleigh. I have been trailed from work, within my home, and elsewhere across the Triangle. A third party Lebanese national close to the First Lady, based in the US, has been linked to what I would call "the secret espionage." He was assigned to help coordinate the PI monitoring directed at my person. What's the Lebanese national's objective? Your guess is as good as mine. Thanks for your attention.

Meanwhile, on October 22nd 2012, the GRTS broadcast an interview featuring Editor Pa Nderry M'Bai's parents. Mr. M'Bai's parents rallied their supporter for Jammeh and the APRC. Mr. M'Bai's Mum used the interview to disown the firebrand Editor. She was not happy with Mr. M'Bai's opposition to the Gambian dictator and his regime. The Jammeh PR stunt was aimed at portraying the exiled Editor in the negative light.

Editor M'Bai in his reaction said: "the end justifies the means." He said he was not surprised by his parent's remarks—given the culture of fear in the Gambia. He said his parents spoke out of fear, but no sane parent will disown his son. He branded Mr. Jammeh a delusional fool, who wants to use his parents to market his battered image.

Mr. M'Bai is of the view that Mr. Jammeh's cheap publicity stunt could be a blessing in disguise for him and his Freedom Newspaper media. He said what is happening is: The truth versus deception. He said Jammeh survives on lies and propaganda. Our only crime is for having the audacity to expose Jammeh's lies and crimes against humanity, Editor M'Bai said.

"Today's GRTS broadcast signals that our work here at the Freedom Newspaper is paying off. Our work is having a devastating blow on Jammeh's criminal enterprise. The end justifies the means," Editor M'Bai posited.

It has been gathered that the dismissal of Lamin Waa Juwara, the Regional Minister has to do with his refusal to lead a team of Jammeh agents to interview my parents. Mr. Juwara was sacked the day my parents appeared on GRTS commending the President for his developmental projects for the country. Juwara and my Dad are very good friends. He visits my Dad each time he is in the Niamina area.

My parents were paraded before the national television GRTS to disassociate themselves from my journalistic work. The GRTS program was pre-arraigned. They spoke against my opposition to Jammeh and his APRC regime. The entire nation was shocked by the regime's desperate attempts to drag my innocent parents into their cheap propaganda.

CHAPTER THIRTEEN

THE MOST SIGNIFICANT EVENTS IN US'S HISTORY

Abstract: This paper discusses the most significant events in the United States' political history. The author covered a wide range of issues on his final project paper-ranging from the genesis of the Cold War era, McCarthyism, the Civil Rights Movement, the Vietnam War, the Watergate scandal, and the much talked about corporate greed. The author also provides a detailed account about the factors that triggered the Cold War. He also commented on the US Foreign Relations shift. This was one of the papers I presented before my graduation at the University of Phoenix.

Introduction: The United States, Britain, and Russia were in alliance during the World War II, which led to the defeat of Germany, and its former ally Japan. The alliance was reached in the spirit of ending Hitler's western domination. Many lives were lost in that bloody war, which ravages Europe, and its surroundings.

Having successfully fought the war, the US and the Soviet Union (Russia) became strange bed fellows, following what observers call Russia's growing military might. The USSR was competing with the United States in terms of nuclear weapons. Russia had atomic bombs, and other deadly missiles, which poses a major threat to the United State's national security. Russia was in the position to conquer many Western countries militarily, thanks to its military might.

Even well before the World War II alliance merger, the United States has always distrusted Russia. The US at the time believed that the Soviet Union was posed to undermine its national security, through the release of weapons of mass destruction. The US entertained the belief that Russia was recruiting foreign spies to tap its military capabilities. This to some extent had strained the relationship between the two superpowers.

The United States was also concerned about Russia's growing power dominance. The USSR had been propagating for communism, which does not go down well with the United States. While the US advocates for the promotion of democratic culture, on the other hand, Russia was busy promoting communism. One could safely argue that the issue of communism also triggered the Cold War era. The USSR became popular, as it succeeds in initiating communism in other Western countries. "The Soviets had gotten Hungary's Joszef Cardinal Mindszenty, an outspoken anti-communist, to confess to espionage, and they also seemed to be able to indoctrinate political enemies and even control the thoughts of entire populations (Stephen Budiansky Stephen, Goode E. Erica, Gest Ted 1994).

Politics in the United States during the 50s was characterized by an environment of fear, and uncertainty. Take for example, the McCarthyism era, which contributed to a nationwide fear. All these, was done in the name of fighting communism.

The McCarthyism era undermines the United States' much cherished political freedoms. McCarthyism was more of a witch hunting spree aimed at targeting suspected communist, and socialism supporters, or sympathizers. The whole idea of McCarthyism was to wage an anti communist crusade, which Republican Senator R McCarthy, of Wisconsin, and his group partly succeeded to some extent. The Colorado website reported that "McCarthyism and the political and cultural anti-communist hysteria it created threatened the American's basic rights."

The era of McCarthyism was also characterized by the sacking of suspected disloyal workers. Workers suspected of having ties with

Communist regimes were dismissed, and in some occasions prosecuted. The majority of the list of the suspected communist spies, supposedly on the State Department payroll, and was submitted to the Federal Bureau of Investigations (FBI), by Senator McCarthy for scrutiny was later found to be false. Mr. McCarthy could not prove his allegations against the accused persons.

While climate of fear continues to grip Democrats, many people at the time were afraid to speak out against the Government-for fear of being labeled a communist. The consequences were dire so to speak. Take, for example the sentencing to death of two couple Ethel and Julius Rosenberg, who were accused of spying. The allegations were that the couples were supplying state secrets to the communist regime.

Granted, espionage is a serious crime, but sentencing the couple to death was a violation of their right to live. Laws barring accused persons the right to innocence until proven guilty also undermined the right to a fair trial. All accused persons are presumed innocent until proven guilty by a court of law. Convicts should also be availed with the opportunity to exhaust all legal remedies before being sentenced to death.

The burning down of Government libraries, suspected of containing subversive materials by Senator McCarthy and his group was also an affront to free speech and democracy. The Voice of America Radio, and other media outlets were targeted in that random raid of suspected media houses possessing communist documents. Mr. McCarthy's attempts to screen out suspected communists supporters serving the United States army were also aimed sowing seeds of discord amongst the military.

The passage of the Loyalty Act also marked the screening of teachers, and other Federal workers in this country. Like, the McCarthyism theory, the loyalty act was also aimed at curbing suspected communist spies in Government. Federal workers were obliged to take an oath indicating that they will be loyal to the United States Government. McCarthyism advocates for anti communism, and socialism.

The formation of the Civil rights Group was triggered by the racial segregation, discrimination and injustices in the country. There were racial imbalances or injustices at the time. Minority groups, mainly blacks, and the Latino population were being segregated, and discriminated against.

Concerned by the lack of racial equality in the country, the Civil Rights Movement decided to spearhead nationwide protest marches to resist against what they called at the time white supremacy, and racial discrimination. The Civil Rights struggle was greeted with violence, and killings. Many lost their lives during the cause of fighting the racial injustices taking place in the country.

While the likes of Martin Luther King junior used the streets to vent their anger against racial injustices, the case of Oliver Brown is still fresh in our minds. Mr. Brown used the judicial system to fight racial segregation in our school system. Brown could not come into term, as to how his own daughter could not attend white schools in her neighborhood.

Initial attempts to contest the legality of such racial segregation were dismissed by the courts, but following a subsequent appeal, he was granted victory. He won the case.

Like Mr. Brown, Rosa Parks also suffered the same racial discrimination. She was jailed for merely refusing to give up her bus seat. Ms. Parks' case attracted a nationwide demonstration, as blacks decided to boycott public transportation in protest.

These, among other racial discrimination cases were recorded at the time. Blacks were denied white collar jobs, decent housing among other social needs. They were confined to rural areas. The Daily News quoted President Obama as saying that ""there's probably never been less discrimination in America than there is today." Still, he said, "make no mistake: the pain of discrimination is still felt in America."

President Kennedy also played an important role in recognizing the existence of the Civil Rights Movement. Prior to his killing, Kennedy's government assured the Civil rights activists that discrimination would not be tolerated. He made efforts to pass anti discrimination legislation, which was later finalized by his successor. The Civil rights Movement was also officially recognized, while white supremacy was discouraged at all levels.

President Richard Nixon's Cold War foreign policy strategies were unique, in the sense that he was able to win the hearts and minds of America's former arch rivals-notably the Soviet Union. With the support of his dynamic National Security adviser Henry Kissinger, President Nixon was able to promote a major foreign policy shift, this time from peace containment diplomacy, instead of the usage of arms to tackle its perceived rivals. The Nixon administration was able to reach a bi-lateral deal with the soviets in the area of arms manufacturing. For example, there was a nuclear arms concession reached, which was aimed at containing the soviets from expanding its military might. The Nixon administration at the time wanted the soviets to reduce its nuclear exploration program.

Mr. Nixon's new diplomacy initiative duped as the "China Card" was also a success story. He was able to penetrate communist nation China, despite years of hostility with the United States. The United States had pledged to restore diplomatic ties with China during Nixon's era. Mr. Nixon himself was a strong opponent of communism, but he decided to engage United State's perceived enemies-most importantly communist nations into a peaceful dialogue.

The whole purpose of the US/China diplomatic relation was aimed at weakening other rival communist countries-notably the soviets. China emerging as a major new economic power, might likely sends a mixed signals to its communist neighbors. Therefore, the US believed that by winning the support of China, it would succeed in neutralizing other communist nations.

President Nixon's visit to China and Moscow were all part of the new peace deal initiated by his administration. The new deal was aimed at promoting trade between the respective countries, and also the containment of nuclear expansion. His Government's role in restoring peace in Vietnam was clearly manifested in his new foreign policy deal, even though his government supported Southern Vietnam at the time.

The Watergate scandal marked the end of President Nixon's political career. In other words, it was a test for the United State's much cherished democracy, because lawmakers were able to act on time to arrest the power abuses, obstruction of justice, and political persecution going on in the country, during Nixon's era. It also helps to promote transparency, accountability, and probity-most importantly check and balances within government.

President Richard Nixon was never impeached per say. Upon realizing the implications of his continued presence in office, following the Watergate scandal, he decided to resign ahead of time to avoid impeachment. President Nixon was aware of the possible embarrassment the said proposed impeachment proceedings were going to have on his person, and party. He has no alternative, but to call it quits.

The Watergate scandal exposes the amount of power abuse perpetrated during Nixon's era. In the first place, it was wrong for a government, which was expected to protect, and safeguards its citizens to be named in such a scandal. Therefore, if the government is seen to be aiding and abetting agents of crime, it would lose the trust, and confidence of the very people it sought to protect. Public trust is essential in any democratic dispensation. In the absence of trust, nothing will work.

Obstruction of justice is a serious crime. And based on the information available on the course material, this was evident during Nixon's administration. Witnesses lied on oath just to exonerate Nixon, and others in government. The government also tried to meddle into judicial activities. This was evident in the appointment of judges. Concerns were raised over the government's impartiality in the way it appoints judges. Nixon tends to appoint judges, whom he thinks will serve his government's interest.

The Watergate scandal is still fresh in the minds of Americans. Power corrupt, absolute power corrupt. The United States is a free country, and therefore, dissent should be nurtured at all cost.

During Nixon's era, anti war protesters, civil right activists, and other political movements were prosecuted. One thing, the Watergate scandal teaches us is that impunity, and tyranny does not last. Leaders should be accountable to its people.

The Vietnamese war was greeted with strong opposition across the country. Students across the US believe that such a war was a waste of resources, and as well as an affront to the very democratic principles, the United States had stood for. In other words, many argued that the US stepped its bounds by waging a war against Vietnam, when there were pressing issues of national importance to be tackled. For example, the average American at the time wanted job, healthcare, decent housing, college education, and guaranteed national security. Anything short of this was considered unacceptable to the nation's much cherished democracy.

The Vietnamese war was triggered by the growing expansion of communism in Asia. The US Government at the material time believe that Vietnam was likely to team up with its arch rivals-notably communist nations such as China, and Russia to undermines its national security capabilities. China and Russia were at the time lobbying support from other communist nations to strengthen its military might. The former Soviet Union was also posed to introduce communism in the United States, with reports of the recruitment of soviet spies to penetrate the US national security apparatus. The soviets were committed to unseating the existing US Government and replacing it with a communist regime.

Concerned by such developments, the United States deemed it imperative to engage the Vietnamese Northern communist regime military. The US, in alliance with the Southern Vietnamese regime, fought their allies in the Northern region. The whole purpose of the war was to end communism in Vietnam. The US backed the Southern Vietnamese by providing them with military support, and other economic incentives. Countries perceived to be communist supporters were excluded from us financial, and military aid.

Even though, the Communist regime in the Northern Vietnam, never poses as a major security threat to the United States, but the Government wanted to take control of it, in order to weaken the growing communist expansion in Asia. Although, on the other hand, many were with the view that there was no justification for the said war.

Tensions started to mount nationwide, following the growing number of US causalities in the Vietnamese war. The world digital history reported that "The Vietnam War cost the United States 58,000 lives and 350,000 casualties. It also resulted in between one and two million Vietnamese deaths." There was public outrage throughout the country, following rise death toll. Students, community leaders, and right activists voiced their opposition against the war.

The advent of television also tends to influence the student's involvement in the anti war protest. The news media portrayed scary pictures of death US soldiers in their evening newscast. This, to some extent, had influenced public perception towards the rationale behind such a war. Many believe that the war should not have happened in the first place. They questioned the motive behind the Government's action.

In registering their dissatisfaction against the Government's move, students organized protest marches in many colleges across the country. The Kent State protest tragedy in Ohio is still fresh in minds of Americans. The anti war riots, left many students killed, and a massive destruction to public property. The National Guards fired, and killed students' protesters. There was a growing hostility between the military, and civilian population. Students never appreciated the fact that the soldiers were acting on a government order to fight in Vietnam. They tend to develop a different perception towards the military, and the entire government machinery.

The Vietnam War being seen as waste of government resources. Many believe that the funds that were used to fight the war could have been challenged to pressing developmental sectors, which were in dire need of attention. Americans wanted jobs, welfare, and a good healthcare system.

When President Richard Nixon decided to extend the war to Cambodia, there was a growing opposition to his move. Many believe that he was embarking on a lost battle since the Northern Vietnamese regime were yet to be concurred militarily by the US forces on the ground. Many viewed his move as uncalled for, amid a nationwide protest to ask for the withdrawal of the US troops from Vietnam. "Richard Nixon became the next president, and his war strategy included increasing the air war over North Vietnam, extending the war into Laos and Cambodia, and slowly bringing the troops home (Caruso Kevin).

The students unrest had some economic, political and security ramifications. For example, there was a significant lost of public property, and lives. Economic activities were stalled, thanks to the anti war riots. This, to some extent, undermined businesses. In the absence of relative peace, there cannot be meaningful development.

On the other hand, the Government also lost public confidence, following what was considered as the unjustified war, and the killing of the student protesters. Many condemned the killings. Unprovoked national guards shot and killed students. They argued that the students were merely exercising their rights to freedom of association.

The news of the students killing sent shocking waves across the country. Many criticized the US security forces. They argue that soldiers have betrayed the oath they have taken-that is to protect the lives and properties of Americans. Tempers flared up across the US.

Civil rights activist Martin Luther King was also in the forefront in waging an anti war campaign. Like the students, Dr. King too was opposed to the Vietnamese war. He questioned the rationale behind the war. Dr. King had spearheaded so many anti war protest marches.

While President Nixon was not the pioneer of the Vietnamese war, it is imperative to note that he also played a major role in trying to liberate the Southern Vietnamese. Despite public criticism against his Government's policies towards Vietnam, Nixon was determined to engage the Northern communist regime. He ensured that US troops stayed in Vietnam to fight the war

Having realized that it was practically impossible to defeat the Northern Vietnamese communist regime military, the US Government under the leadership of President Nixon decided to embark on a major diplomatic shift. This time, they initiated what was called at the time a containment program. The whole purpose of the containment program was to win the support of communist regimes-notably China, and Russia by extending peace deal diplomacy to them.

The Nixon administration registered significant achievements in their quest to meant fences with their perceived arch rivals. With the support of his National Security adviser Henry Kissinger, President Nixon was able to reach a peace deal with communist nations such as China and Russia. Chief among his Government's demands were the reduction of the manufacturing of nuclear weapons by communist nations. The US also agreed to promote bilateral trade with its allies, with the ultimate aim of ending communist expansion.

The administration of President Reagan recorded a major economic success during its term in office. Inflation was brought to a minimal level, while the economy was growing steadily. The job market boomed overtime. The Charismatic, and outspoken US President was able to restore the US economy on track, following years of recession.

President Reagan's economic success story could be attributed to his sound economic policies. His Government passed legislations, such as the Economic Recovery Program in a bid to curb inflation, and other economic challenges facing the nation. Reagan's famous tax cut policy helped to stimulate the economy to some extent. There was also judicious management of state resources under Mr. Reagan's watch. Unnecessary government spending was discouraged during his watch.

Besides, the economic reform legislations spearhead by his administration, the Reagan government also promotes liberal economy. The Government at the time ensured that local businesses were given free hand to run their show. Mr. Reagan refuses to enforce price control mechanism, or other methods employed by other regimes to curb inflation. Instead, he promotes free trade, tax reduction, healthcare, and sound economic policies.

Thanks to President Reagan's blueprint economic policies, the American economy boomed. Unemployment was low during his watch, while wages went up. There were jobs all over the country. One could safely argue that his administration was very instrumental in actualizing the much talked about American dream. Regan extended Amnesty to the millions of illegal Immigrants residing in the US. This to some extent helped to beef up the nation's workforce. Some of the Immigrants had different working background.

President Reagan was able to get the support of some conservatives into his party. His administration was also committed to promoting religious tolerance. Mr. Reagan was a strong opponent of the Soviet Union. He was also opposed to communism.

President Ronald Reagan's Reaganomics program had its positive and negative consequences. While it was aimed at tax reduction, combating inflation, judicious management of state resources, reducing Government spending, and corporation regulation, on the other hand the program created some degree of poverty disparity in the country. The program elevated the economic status of the rich and corporate America. For example, the poor were marginalized, and discriminated against in terms of access to white collar jobs. The majority of the white collar jobs went to the white population.

Corporate greed also created massive unemployment, and homelessness. There was also cheap labor. American jobs were also being outsourced overseas during President Reagan's watch. Moody reported that "Business put politics on an open class basis in the '70s when it declared 'one-sided class war."

While Reagan's tax policy was widely hailed, many Americans believed that the policy was meant to advance the economic needs of the rich, and the influential business community. Big corporations exploited the labor market by providing cheap wages to the workforce.

There have been numerous economic and political transformations in the United States. Despite previous economic challenges befalling this country, the US economy emerged stronger and vibrant during

Reagan, and Clinton's eras. The nation continues to witness economic prosperity.

With judicious management of state resources, America's future would be bright. Initiating major economic reforms, might also impact positively towards the nation's economic future. The path for economy recovery should start now. Failure of which, might have some long term economic ramifications on the ailing economy.

References:

Caruso Kevin. The Vietnam War. Retrieved From: http://www.vietnammemorial.com/vietnam-war.html

Learn about the Vietnam War. Retrieved June 20 2009 From:http://www.digitalhistory.uh.edu/modules.cfm

http://www.colorado.edu/AmStudies/lewis/2010/mccarthy.htm

Stephen Budiansky Stephen, Goode E. Erica, Gest Ted. (January 24 1994) The Cold War experiments. Retrieved May 23 2009 From: http://www.geocities.com/area51/shadowlands/6583/project120.html

Saul Michale. (July 16, 2009) President Obama honors civil rights pioneers with speech at NAACP centennial convention http://www.nydailynews.com/news/politics/2009/07/16/2009-07-16_president_obama_honors_civil_rights_pioneers_with_speech_at_naacp_centennial_con.html

Moody Kim. Reagan, The business Agenda and the collapse of labor. Retrieved July 16 2009 From: http://66.102.1.104/scholar?q=cache:rSF4wJWzfj4J:scholar.google.com/+corporate+greed+during+Reagan&hl=en

CHAPTER FOURTEEN

END IMPUNITY IN THE GAMBIA

The impoverished nation of The Gambia, is currently witnessing an untold human rights, social and political crisis. Faced by political and economic uncertainties, the Gambia is the scene for extra judicial killings, cold blooded murders, abductions, arrest and the torture of political opponents. The country is on the brink of total collapse, in view of Gambia's worsening rights and political crisis. Africa's most ruthless and brutal dictator Yahya Jammeh is ruling the tiny West African country with impunity, showing little, or no respect for the rule of law and basic freedoms of the country's citizenry.

Since coming to power in July of 1994, Mr. Jammeh has been constantly undermining the country's constitution, with the sole objective of entrenching his leadership. He pioneered all kinds of draconian laws, ranging from the setting up the National Media Commission, the infamous Indemnity Bill and the Local Government Act.

While the National Media Commission was aimed at the muzzling the private press, the Indemnity Act, gave license to Gambia's security forces to shoot and kill citizens without having the fear of being arraigned before any court of law. The indemnity Act also gave sweeping powers to the President to pardon member of the security forces, who were accused of killing dozens of Gambian students in April of 2000. The students were protesting against the killing of their colleague Ebrima Barry. Barry was allegedly beaten to death by the personnel of the Brikama Fire and Ambulance Services. The following students were killed by Gambia's security forces.

1. Baboucarr Badjie, Talinding Arabic School

2. Wuyai Foday Mansareh, Anglican Institute

3. Momodou Lamin Chune, Latrikunda Junior Secondary school

4. Momodou Lamin Njie GTTI

5. Claesco Pierra, New Jewswang Secondary school,

6. Karomo Barrow ICE High school

7. Regional Carrol

8. Lamin A Bojang

9. Ousman Sabally, Brikamaba

10. Sainey Nyabally, Brikamaba

11. Bamba Jobarteh, Armitage Senior Secondary School

12. Unidentified teenager killed

13. Abdoulie Sanyang

14. Omar Barrow, former journalist/Red Cross Volunteer was also shot dead.

The amended Local Government Act empowered the President to fire elected Mayors and other Local Government leaders in the country. The President also reserves the right to dissolve Municipal Councils anytime he deems it necessary. The passage of the Local Government Act, signals the end of free and fair elections in The Gambia. Voters are being stripped off their constitutional guaranteed right to elect their local leaders. The President has been empowered by law to overrule such powers. He can fire local leaders without cause.

From 1994 to date, Jammeh has been ruling The Gambia with an iron-fist. There are many unresolved murders in The Gambia. The state, which is often suspected as the prime suspect, in such atrocities, had never demonstrated any interest, or commitment to bringing the killers of such citizens to book. A classical case was the murder of the founding Editor of the Banjul based Point Newspaper, Deyda Hydara. Since the murder of Hydara in December of 2004, there have not been any serious investigations conducted by this administration. The Government instead came up with a bogus confidential report, in which it tried to blackmail the slain editor.

Another blood bath hits The Gambia in July of 2005, when President Jammeh allegedly instructed the killing of 60 West African Immigrants, 40 of whom were Ghanaians. The immigrants were mistaken as dissident rebels poised to disrupt the country's ailing democratic process. The following Security officials were allegedly linked to the killing of the Ghanaians.

1. Major Musa Jammeh—Deceased

2. Captain Tumbul Tamba—Deceased

3. Ousman Sonko-Interior Minister

4. Staff Sergeant Sanna Manjang—Active Duty

5. Staff Sergeant Malick Jatta—Active Duty

6. Lieutenant Kawsu Camara, alias Bombaredeh—Active Duty

7. Other unnamed State Guard Solders.

In March of 2006, the government also allegedly summarily executed five senior Gambian security officials, who were suspected of having hands in the March abortive coup, led by the erstwhile army Chief Colonel Ndure Cham. The following officers were allegedly executed by the Government without any form of legal recourse:

1. Daba Marena, former Director General of the National Intelligence Agency

2. Lt. Ebou Lowe,

3. 2nd Lt. Alieu Ceesay

4. Warrant Officer Alpha Bah

5. Staff Sgt. Manlafi Corr.

In a press release issued shortly before the killing of the former service chiefs, the government claimed that the men escaped while being escorted to a jail house in the Central River Division. It came up with the said story, in a bid to conceal the killing of the above mentioned former security chiefs. Sources close to the Army Command said the men were executed in grand style by personnel of the State Guards, known as the jungullars.

Journalist Ebrima Chief Manneh has been missing for over five years now. There are fears that Manneh must have been allegedly secretly executed by the government. His family, the Gambian local media and the Ghana based Media Foundation for West Africa, had launched numerous appeals for the Government to produce the body of the missing journalist without success.

Concerned by Manneh's plight, the Media Foundation filed a court action at the Economic Community of West Africa (ECOWAS) court in Abuja against the Government of The Gambia. The Gambian authorities had openly treated the Sub-regional court with contempt by failing to show up in court to defend the court action. The court later ruled in favor of journalist Manneh. The missing journalist was awarded with a substantial amount money by the court for compensation. The Jammeh regime has failed to settle the pending judgment.

To further catalogue the atrocities committed by the Jammeh administration, it's imperative to cite the unfinished persecution meted out to local journalists—most importantly the Independent Newspaper.

Before the illegal closure of the Independent, the government through its agents at the NIA had systematically tortured Editor Musa Saidykhan and Madi Ceesay. The journalists were accused of publishing articles endangering "National Security."

In addition, following the hacking of the Freedom Newspaper, by agents of The Gambian government, dozens of the paper's subscribers were arrested and tortured by the state. Some workers, whose names appeared on the so called list of the Freedom Newspaper subscribers, were also fired from their jobs, with threats of dragging them to court. An arrest warrant was issued against our former Banjul Bureau Chief. The arrest warrant was aired both on public radio and Television for days. Mr. Bah has since resettled in the United States with his wife.

Armed soldiers were dispatched to get the reporter alive or dead. Other Freedom Newspaper subscribers suffered body pain, as a result of the torture they suffered in the hands of the NIA. This author's family was also routinely persecuted by the Gambian state.

The hackers posted a false statement on the Freedom Newspaper, claiming that Editor Pa Nderry MBai had pledged his allegiance to the Ruling Party and was poised to return home with a former official of the government Ebou Jallow. They also claimed that the list of the subscribers posted on the Freedom Newspaper and the Pro-government Newspaper, the Daily Observer, were Editor MBai's informants.

Their ultimate goal was to smear Mr. M'Bai's credibility as a journalist and also to instill fear into the population. Despite such blackmailing tactics, the Freedom Newspaper is still rattling Jammeh's cage. The paper is more dynamic and popular today than ever before its emergence into media landscape. The paper continues to command its leading role on the cyberspace online journals.

The Government of The Gambia had applied all kinds of censorship mechanism in a bid to ban the Freedom Newspaper in The Gambia. It blocked the paper's main IP address on numerous times. This was contained in the United States State Department Human Rights Report on the Gambia. The most recent case involves the new owners of

GAMTEL, who were unhappy with the paper's reportage of a looming bankruptcy at GATEL. The new owners who reached a partnership with The Gambian Government, has resorted to blocking the Freedom Newspaper IP address in The Gambia.

With all these gross rights violations taking place in The Gambia, Gambia's plight is still a major cause for concern. The International Community is not very much responsive to Gambia's plight. Our people are dying on a daily basis in the hands of the ruthless Gambian dictator. Political oppression and marginalization is the order of the day.

Gambia's case is similar to the Zimbabwean situation. Jammeh and Mugabe shared common characteristics. The two, have been known for their bully foreign policies against the West.

In the case of Zimbabwe, Britain and the United States acted rightly by imposing sanctions against the Mugabe Government. Such sanctions are welcomed because they are geared towards ending impunity in the Southern African country.

We still cannot understand why similar measures are not meted out to the Government of The Gambia. There are enough justifications for sanctions to be imposed against the Jammeh Government.

The liberties and political freedoms of Gambians supersede the interest of President Jammeh and his partners in crime. The Western world should help to restore democracy, rule of law and civility in The Gambia. This can be done in the form of imposing aid sanctions against Jammeh's repressive regime. They can also impose visa restriction against corrupt Gambian officials and their families.

Besides, what's the rationale behind supporting a murderous and corrupt Government, which is not accountable to its citizens. Corruption is endemic in The Gambia today. The President is richer than the state. His sudden riches came as a surprise to many Gambians. Here was a person, whose bank account was almost in the red at the time of the illegal coup, he spearheaded against the deposed Jawara Government.

The Gambia has been ranked among the failed states in Africa by the International Human Index. Institutionalized corruption is hindering economic growth in The Gambia.

The nation's poverty ratio is on the rise, with low life expectancy rate. The average Gambian lives below one dollar a day, while unemployment continues to threaten the lives of the poverty stricken citizens.

The Gambia is a private sector led economy. The Government is not investor friendly. It arrest, detain and deport foreign investors. The latest case involves the Carnegie mining company, whose General Manager has been charged with economic crime by the state. The Jammeh regime has accuses Carnegie of falsifying mining data information. Carnegie denied the allegations. It in turn sued The Gambian Government for breach of contract. The mining company is claiming millions of US dollars against Jammeh Government. The case is pending in the British courts.

Diseases such as Malaria, diabetics and HIV/Aids are on the increase. The President's false claim that he has found cure for aids and diabetics had brought false hope for Gambian aids sufferers.

Despite concerns raised by the United Nations, Medical Scientists and aids activists about the potential implications of Jammeh's false aids cure claims, the President is still insisting that he got cure for aids.

There is no indication at this hour suggesting that President Yahya Jammeh will step down from power in the short term. He has fortified himself with his Jolla ethic group by hiring them into key positions in Government.

Citizens hope for effecting political change, through the ballot box, has been shattered, thanks to Jammeh's direct control of the Electoral Commission. The Electoral Commission dances to the dictates of the President. He hires and fires its official at his own accord. To some extent, this had affected the independence of the Independent Electoral Commission.

The Gambia is at cross-roads. "Jammeh is likely to die violently, because he does not subscribe to the ideals of democratic change of

Government. He undermines the constitution with impunity. The Gambia is on the road to full blown political turmoil. Jammeh is not the type who would relinquish the Presidency like that. He wants to rule for life and shall face the consequences sooner or later. All despots end up in disgrace," A Gambian political observer said.

All efforts should be made to end impunity in The Gambia. Impunity is at its peak in The Gambia. Gambians deserve better life. Impunity breeds lawlessness. The world should act now to salvage the impoverished nation of The Gambia.

The Obama administration should consider championing for a regime change in the Gambia, in a bid to disrupt the activities of some Lebanese Hezbollah financiers in that impoverished West African nation. The current regime in the Gambia is anti US interest. This is evident on the dictator's open embracement of Hezbollah supporters in Banjul. Lebanese businesses linked to financing terrorism have been allowed to operate in that country despite US'S concerns about the implications of harboring such enemies of freedom.

Washington should act expeditiously to protect its own interest before enemies of freedom will strike. Hezbollah is expanding its network in the Gambia at an alarming rate! It is time to act now to protect US interest.

Supporters of terrorist groups normally posed as investors to launder money and in the process, the proceeds derived from such nefarious elicit business activities are wired overnight to Lebanon and elsewhere around the world to their business. Banjul is becoming a fast money laundering ground to expand the Hezbollah network.

The blacklisting of Prime Bank Gambia and its affiliate body in Canada did not stop the Hezbollah supporters from carrying out their callous economic crimes. The group is now using a local Gambian Bank—partly owned by the Gambia Government to evade the US Treasury Department sanctions to wire money to their contacts overseas.

It's imperative to note that the US can only succeed on its War on terror provided that host countries such as the Gambia are willing to cooperate. US Treasury Department sanctions directed at terrorists and their financiers must be enforced both locally and internationally if we want to be much safer from the bad guys. The enforcement of such sanctions requires the support of genuine and sincere Governments around the world.

The Gambian Head of state Yahya Jammeh wants to dine with the people of the United States and Hezbollah supporters at the same time. That's impossible. Jammeh will either dine with freedom loving Americans, or come out from the closet and declare his support for Hezbollah.

Jammeh's apparent silence to act on the recent US Treasury Department report—linking the Tajideen brothers to financing terrorism speaks volume. One would have expected him to initiate an independent investigation into the business activities of the Tajideen brothers in the Gambia, as the Angolans did with the view of taking decisive actions to safeguard the reputation of this country. But for Jammeh, he cannot afford to lose the Tajideens since they are meeting his economic needs. He is behaving as if everything is cool and dandy when the US'S interest is at stake!

The Obama administration should realize that the continued presence of Hezbollah supporters in Banjul will not only undermine US national security, but the safety of its own citizens in that country. Hezbollah needs to be tackled in the Gambia in the interest of global peace!

For this to happen, it requires political will, commitment and dedication on the side of Washington to engage dictator Jammeh into an adult conversation. Mr. Jammeh needs to be told upfront that he is working against US'S interest by allowing the Tajideen brothers and the other Lebanese terrorist supporters to operate in the Gambia. Jammeh also needs to be told that harboring a US enemy tantamount to aiding and abetting. He either play by the democratic card, or be declared a "sworn enemy" of the United States.

Hezbollah supporters have hijacked Gambia's financial system—thanks to the blank check accorded to them by the dictator. The so called investors had infiltrated the local banking industry. They can wire millions of dollars on a single day overseas unmonitored.

Due to the growing culture of corruption in The Gambia, Lebanese businesses linked to Hezbollah bribe their way by having the backing of the state. No one dares question the legitimacy of their illicit business practices. All monetary transactions—be it legitimate or illegitimate are okayed without question.

Besides the growing presence of Hezbollah backers in the Gambia, that country is becoming a hot spot for South American drug cartels. Tons of cocaine is being deposited on the shores of The Gambia by South American planes. Hezbollah normally derived its funds mainly through drug trade and money laundering, according to documented research papers by security experts.

A highly placed source close to Gambia's anti narcotic unit has confided to me that a cousin of the indicted Lebanese brothers was on their radar when the one billion dollar cocaine case was impounded in that country. The Babob Island lodge in Kuloro, which was rented out to the South American drug dealers was built by the Lebanese national.

"When our men made the arrest of the one billion cocaine case, the Lebanese national in question was in Lebanon on a trip. We wanted to invite him for questioning, but he never return to the Gambia since the incident. Lamin Darboe was the manager of the property," said our source.

"The Babob Lodge in Kuloro serves as a control tower for the planes that drop off the Cocaine from South America. This was the place where the crew had their communication gadgets. The property belongs to a Lebanese man related to the Lebanese Hezbollah supporters in the Gambia," my source alleged.

Black listing the Lebanese Canadian bank is not enough; without including local Gambian bank(s) being used at this hour by Hezbollah supporters to evade the US action. The Obama administration must act now in the interest of safeguarding US national security and interest overseas.

CHAPTER FIFTEEN

DR. AMADOU SCATTERED JANNEH SPEAKS

Former Information Minister Dr. Amadou Scattered Janneh, who was jailed for life imprisonment by the dictatorial regime of Yahya Jammeh after been accused of printing t shirts calling for an end to dictatorship in the impoverished West African country is determined to continue with his set agenda to liberate the Gambia from Jammeh's tyranny. Mr. Janneh in an exclusive interview with the Freedom Newspaper, discusses his immediate plans for the Gambia, prison life, an ongoing online discussions spearheaded by Joseph Sambou, AKA Joe Sambou, criticizing him for allowing to align himself with the dictator after abandoning his diasporan colleagues in the struggle. You will also hear Dr. Janneh's reaction to such criticisms. The former Information Minister also lamented about the deplorable prison conditions in the Gambia. "Mile Two is one of the worst prisons in the world. Many prisoners are packed like sardines in overcrowded, disease-ridden cells. The food is extremely poor and inadequate, contributing to malnutrition and other health-related problems. The medical clinic is grossly under equipped and the staff lack basic skills. Most prisoners are allowed only 4 thirty-minute visits per year, while death row inmates and detainees are not allowed any visits at all. We were locked in our cells at Mile 2 for up to 20 hours every day. These many problems have contributed to a very high mortality rate in the prison," said Mr. Janneh. Below is the full text of the interview . . . .

FN: Thanks Dr. Janneh for joining us here at the Freedom Newspaper. It's great to have you as a guest here at Freedom. Could you please briefly introduce yourself to our audience?

Dr. AJ: I was born in Gunjur, Kombo South in 1962. I traveled to the US in January 1983 for further studies, and by December 2000 I earned a Ph.D. in political science from The University of Tennessee. I am married to Mame Fatou, and I have four children.

FN: Could you explain the genesis of the CCG? How do you get involved into the CCG? What inspired you to be part of the group?

Dr. AJ: I was very frustrated with the Gambia's rapid decline and the gross human rights abuses of the Jammeh regime. I wrote articles using pseudonyms, but I got bolder with the successes of the Arab Spring and decided to do something more spectacular. I found like-minded people and the rest is history.

FN: Printing a t shirt calling for an end to dictatorship in the Gambia landed you in jail. You were sentenced to life imprisonment. Could you describe the circumstances surrounding your arrest and imprisonment?

Dr. AJ: It is a long story. In short, I contracted Modou Keita to print 100 t-shirts for me by May 25, 2011 which he did. These were distributed as a way of marking African Liberation Day and as a show of defiance against the Gambian dictator. I was picked up by plain clothes security agents on June 5, 2011 before being subjected to very inhumane treatment for a one-week period. During all this time, I was not allowed access to my lawyer or the US Consul despite persistent requests.

FN: The Government of the Gambia characterizes the CGG as a subversive group. How true is the government's allegations against the CCG?

Dr. AJ: Of course, if you want to topple dictatorship and establish democracy you should expect your actions to be characterized as subversive by the regime. The goal was to subvert repressive rule while sowing the seeds of responsible and responsive government.

FN: Why was the CCG not officially registered in the Gambia as a legitimate Organization like the other existing political parties and organization have done?

Dr. AJ: The political climate does not allow meaningful freedom of assembly or association. Just recently, for instance, a couple of citizens were jailed for requesting permission to demonstrate against the executions of 9 death row inmates. You could imagine what the dictator's reactions would have been to a registration application from a group demanding freedom and an end to dictatorship.

FN: Don't you think it was suicidal on your part to distribute t shirts calling for an end to dictatorship in the Gambia without following any legal framework to back up your actions?

Dr. AJ: It was not suicidal. I am still around! I never expected to be charged with treason and sedition, but my speech at the University of The Gambia on ALD 2011 calling on Gambians to shed their fears and stand up to Jammeh's tyranny underscored my resolve to speak out.

FN: Have you tried to register the CCG in the Gambia?

Dr. AJ: It was pointless. Our application would have been rejected without a doubt. Do you believe President Jammeh would allow registration of a group demanding serious investigations into forced disappearances, torture by security agents, the killings of students and journalists, etc.?

FN: Don't you think in the absence of a legal framework recognizing the CCG as a registered organization in the Gambia, you are breaking the law?

Dr. AJ: If the government shuts all doors for groups and individuals to operate freely while it continues its repression, setting up an unregistered organization dedicated to nonviolent change is the least one could do.

FN: Your critics opined that given your educational background and past affiliation with the Jammeh administration, it was inexcusable on your part to be associated with a non registered group, majority of whose membership are in exile. How would you react to such criticism?

Dr. AJ: I believe I have already addressed this question.

FN: Why don't you form a political party if you had truly wanted to end dictatorship in the Gambia?

Dr. AJ: Political parties play a crucial role in bringing about change. So do civil society organizations and interest groups. We chose to operate as a nonpartisan civil society group.

FN: Oh you wanted the Egyptian type of revolution to take place in the Gambia?

Dr. AJ: The Gambia is not exactly Egypt. But we won't mind if popular pressure can force our unpopular and autocratic leader from power.

FN: What did you intend to achieve by distributing t shirts to Gambians?

Dr. AJ: It was a show of defiance and a means to erode the enormous fear President Jammeh has successfully cultivated in The Gambian people.

FN: Have you ever anticipated that you would be arrested for merely distributing t shirts calling for the end of Jammeh's regime?

Dr. AJ: Oh, yes! But I never expected to be charged with any wrong doing. I figured that I would be detained for a week and then released. As the government tightened the squeeze to teach me a lesson, I grew even more committed to striving for freedom.

FN: What happen during the course your detention and trial?

Dr. AJ: I was subjected to a great deal of psychological torture, in addition to the common problems that prisoners face in the country—food deprivation, inadequate access to medical care, constant humiliation, etc.

FN: Was your E-mail hacked into by the police investigators?

Dr. AJ: Only my hotmail account was hacked successfully, but it gave the police access to a CCG colleague's account. He had sent his password to that account of mine.

FN: Tell us something about the situation of inmates at Mile Two?

Dr. AJ: Mile Two is one of the worst prisons in the world. Many prisoners are packed like sardines in overcrowded, disease-ridden cells. The food is extremely poor and inadequate, contributing to malnutrition and other health-related problems. The medical clinic is grossly under equipped and the staff lack basic skills. Most prisoners are allowed only 4 thirty-minute visits per year, while death row inmates and detainees are not allowed any visits at all. We were locked in our cells at Mile 2 for up to 20 hours every day. These many problems have contributed to a very high mortality rate in the prison.

FN: Do you have fan in your cell?

Dr. AJ: Are you kidding? Definitely No!

FN: How often inmates die in prison?

Dr. AJ: I know that the Security Wing at Mile 2 Prison with 150 inmates registers on average one death every month, mostly due to preventable diseases. As an indication, 2 of the people on death row died during the second week of this month (October 2012).

FN: Where were you when the first batch of the nine death row inmates were executed?

Dr. AJ: They were executed on August 23, 2012. I was in prison at the time, in the same Wing as the male death row prisoners.

FN: Who is prisoner Lamin Darboe?

Dr. AJ: He was one of those who were executed. As the prisoners were being herded away, he screamed my name a couple of times before being silenced. Mr. Darboe had spent more than a quarter century behind bars before he was killed.

FN: Has all the executed inmates exhausted their appeal processes before their execution?

Dr. AJ: I can say for certain that not all of them exhausted their appeals. For example, Dawda Bojang's case never reached the Gambia Supreme Court. And Malang Sonko was convicted of murder just 8 months earlier. He never faced appeal judges of any kind.

FN: What role have you played in providing information to the outside world about the executions?

Dr. AJ: I made sure the world knew what was taking place.

FN: The government of the Gambia claimed that the inmates were killed through firing squad. Do you buy the regime's story?

Dr. AJ: I cannot say for certain how the executions were carried out, but I am convinced that some form of lethal injection was administered on Thursday, August 23, 2012 after 9:30 p.m.

FN: Do we have people detained at Mile Two without being charged or tried in the courts?

Dr. AJ: There were several detainees at Mile 2. Presently, the longest serving detainees are Abdourahmane Balde, a resident of Tambacounda, Senegal, and M.B. Sarr, a former Naval Commander. Balde has been held without charge since July 1997, and I believe Sarr was arrested in 2006.

FN: What was your worst moment in prison?

Dr. AJ: Hearing Mr. Lamin B.S. Darboe calling my name as he was being taken to be executed.

FN: Did you regret going to prison?

Dr. AJ: I did not regret demanding Freedom and calling for an end to dictatorship in The Gambia.

FN: How did you secure your freedom?

Dr. AJ: I was told my release and subsequent expulsion resulted from Rev. Jesse Jackson's appeals to Yahya Jammeh. But I truly believe it resulted from the sustained campaigns against the regime's repression and calls for my unconditional release.

FN: Have you ever dreamt in your lifetime that Jesse Jackson will be your savior in prison?

Dr. AJ: No. I was pleasantly surprised that one of my role models had anything to do with my release.

FN: What happen after your release?

Dr. AJ: We were taken from Mile 2 to the airport under heavy armed guard and then handed over to Rev. Jackson.

FN: What happen at the airport?

Dr. AJ: We met some government officials, such as Njogu Bah and Lamin Jobarteh—both cabinet ministers. My family members also came to the airport to see me off. It took two hours of negotiations between Jackson and government officials before I could see my mother and other family members.

FN: Who paid for your one way ticket to America?

Dr. AJ: My one-way fare from Banjul to New York on business class was paid for by the Gambia Government (I.e. Yahya Jammeh) at a cost of about US$5,500.

FN: Was any condition attached to your release?

Dr. AJ: We were not allowed to take any flight transiting through Dakar, Senegal.

FN: Jammeh has declared you unwelcomed to the Gambia. Are you traumatized by the president's decision to deport you from your own country?

Dr. AJ: Not at all. It has only strengthened my resolve to work for his exit.

FN: You used to be an arch critic of President Jammeh before returning home to work with his government. What motivated you to go home?

Dr. AJ: I did not return home to work for the government. My father was seriously ill, and as the firstborn I felt a need to be with him at his time of need. After all, I had already spent 20 years (1993-2003) in the US. Unfortunately, he passed away just a month after my return. My first job upon going back was with the US Embassy.

FN: You used to work at the American Embassy before joining the Jammeh regime. Why do you accept to work with President Jammeh's government?

Dr. AJ: I sincerely believed I had a chance to make a difference even if I held office very briefly.

FN: Critics like Joseph Sambou said you betrayed the struggle by abandoning your colleagues in the diaspora to work with Jammeh. Your reaction Sir?

Dr. AJ: The beauty of democracy is that criticism is a normal part of the political process. People have the right to criticize for whatever reason. By the same token, the French say "Bien fait et laissez dire." In essence, do your best and let others criticize.

FN: But the million dollar question many people are asking is: How could you reconcile your actions by accepting to work with a dictatorship when you have written extensively on the Gambia L—denouncing Jammeh and his regime. How genuine were you to reconcile with Jammeh?

Dr. AJ: There was no such thing as reconciliation. I never swayed an inch from my principles, and that is well known.

FN: Has money or love for government position influence your decision to work with the Jammeh government?

Dr. AJ: Not at all. I earned more money both before joining government and after I resumed private economic activity.

FN: At the time of joining Jammeh's regime has anything changed on the status quo? I am talking about governance.

Dr. AJ: I don't quite understand this question. But it is evident that the regime's repressive character has increased in intensity over the years.

FN: The likes of Joe Sambou are asking for an apology from you since you have been "used and abused" by dictator Jammeh. Will you ever apologize to Gambians for having worked with Jammeh?

Dr. AJ: If I was "used and abused" by Jammeh I thought I deserved an apology from him.

FN: Now that you are back in the streets, what will be your main agenda?

Dr. AJ: I am part of CCG /CSAG, and our main task is to unify the various Gambian political groupings and civil society organizations to combat Jammeh's dictatorship and establish real democracy in The Gambia. Along the way we are determined to fight for prisoners' rights, freedom of expression, and investigations into all mysterious killings and disappearances.

FN: Joe Sambou also said that you do not speak for him in your quest to change the dictatorship in Banjul. He said you are a wrong person to champion for change since you allowed yourself to be used by the dictator in the name of nation building. Your views Sir?

Dr. AJ: I have never claimed to speak for anyone. And I am not engaged in a beauty contest. If you have seen the suffering and deaths I have witnessed, you would expend all your energies toward bringing about change and not worry about such categorizations.

FN: Are you still determined to set up a radio station in Dakar?

Dr. AJ: Of course. It is a CCG project. Stay tuned.

FN: What was it like to be an Information Minister under Jammeh's rule?

Dr. AJ: It was very difficult. Yahya Jammeh only likes folks who worship him. Anything short isn't enough. He wants journalists to become mere mouthpieces of his, reporting his every sneeze and cough as important news. Rather than respond to issues raised by journalists, he simply targets them through violence and intimidation.

FN: What was your toughest moment while working with President Jammeh?

Dr. AJ: My toughest moments were when the president flip flopped after endorsing my policy recommendations within my domain.

FN: Do you have any regrets for working with the APRC government?

Dr. AJ: No. It served a purpose.

FN: What transpired between you and Minister Lamin Jobarteh at the Ivory Coast rights conference?

Dr. AJ: Minister Jobarteh gave a very inaccurate and distorted picture of the human rights situation in The Gambia. I was given the opportunity to set the record straight and I seized it. He felt so humiliated at the session that he refused to shake my hand afterwards. But it showed me that I accomplished something that day.

FN: Any last word?

Dr. AJ: Given the enormous challenges we face as Gambians, I believe it is incumbent upon us all to set aside our peripheral differences and focus our energies on dislodging Yahya Jammeh from the helm. The more we bicker amongst ourselves, the longer and harder it would become for us to succeed. The time to unite is now as Jammeh's exit is imminent.

FN: Thanks Dr. Janneh for taking your time to speak to us. Good luck on your future endeavors.

Dr. AJ: I thank you for giving me this opportunity.

ABOUT THE AUTHOR

Pa Nderry M'Bai, is a naturalized Gambian American Investigative journalist based in Raleigh North Carolina. Mr. M'Bai is also the Founding Managing Editor, and Publisher of the US based online Freedom Newspaper INC. The Freedom Newspaper is Gambia's leading, and most authoritative online newspaper—which covers a wide range of issues—most importantly matters relating to Gambian politics, human rights, Governance, official graft, crimes, health, and other human interesting stories. The paper is widely sourced, and quoted by reputable institutions interested in Gambian affairs—thanks to the paper's trademark for its uncompromising editorial policy, and honest reporting without any form of biased, or prejudice. It is widely regarded as Gambia's main source of uncensored news, balanced, and authoritative news medium.

Mr. M'Bai used to work with the Banjul based Daily Observer Newspaper, before moving to the Point Newspaper, where he worked, until his resettlement to the United States in July of 2004. While in The Gambia, Mr. M'Bai, also worked with the Washington based Voice of America Radio Africa Service as its Banjul Correspondent.

Mr. M'Bai also manages an online Internet Radio called Freedom Radio Gambia. Freedom Radio serves as an outlet for the oppressed Gambian Community both at home and abroad, where people freely express their views on issues relating to governance, human rights, the rule of law, and dictator Jammeh's power excesses.

In addition to its rich news program segments, Freedom Radio also provides its audience with an in-depth commentaries, and expert analysis on the situation of Governance in the Gambia. Freedom Radio attracts a huge audience. The radio attracts close to millions of listeners every month. Across Africa, Europe, and America listen to Freedom Radio. It's Gambia's leading online Internet Radio.

Mr. M'Bai suffered numerous arrest and persecution while practicing as a journalist in the Gambia. He used to be the Secretary General of the Gambia Press Union, the country's main press body. Mr. M'Bai was also among the team of Gambian journalists, who fought tirelessly against the draconian Media Commission Bill passed by the Jammeh regime. The new media law was basically aimed at ending press freedom in the Gambia. Journalists, who failed to register with the Commission, risked being penalized, or having their media houses closed.

Mr. M'Bai and his colleagues in the Gambian media worked tirelessly to have the law repealed. Gambian Journalists are no longer required to register with the bogus Media Commission. The regime was compelled to set aside the bad law.

After the completion of his Secondary Education, Mr. M'Bai bagged a degree in Mass Communication with honors from the Arizona based University of Phoenix in 2009. Mr. M'Bai, is an expert on Sene-Gambian related issues. He has written extensively on matters relating to Gambian domestic politics, political developments in Africa, and elsewhere around the world. Mr. M'Bai had in the past granted press interviews to leading news outlets such as the British Broadcasting Corporation (BBC), America's National Public Radio (NPR) and the Voice of America Radio Africa Service Radio (VOA).

Barely five months after his arrival in the US, Mr. M'Bai's Managing Editor Deyda Hydara was shot and killed allegedly by Gambia's security agents. Mr. Hydara was killed on December 16th 2004, immediately after officiating his newspaper's thirteen years anniversary. The incident, which sparked both local and international outcry, left two other female staffers of the Point Newspaper injured. The staffers were riding with Mr. Hydra, when the gunmen ambushed Mr. Hydara's vehicle.

In his book titled: "THE UNTOLD DICTATOR YAHYA JAMMEH'S STORY." Mr. M'Bai exposes the alleged secret murders, economic crimes, gross rights violations, money laundering, and other domestic terrorism activities perpetrated under the regime of the Gambian tyrant Yahya Jammeh since coming to power in July of 1994. Mr. M'Bai's book also discusses Mr. Jammeh's childhood days in rural Gambia, and his emergence into Gambia's political landscape. The Gambia becoming a drug hub nation also featured prominently on Mr. M'Bai's book.

After months of intensive investigations into the murder of Deyda Hydara, Mr. M'Bai was able to uncover the people allegedly behind the murder of Mr. Hydara after interviewing multiple credible sources. Army Major Sanna Manjang, and Regimental Sergeant Major Malick Jatta have been accused of allegedly murdering Mr. Deyda Hydara.

Mr. M'Bai's goal is to relate Gambia's untold story—most importantly state sponsored crimes allegedly committed by a murderous regime in the face of gross human rights violations. Journalists in the Gambia are operating under very difficult conditions. They are battling with draconian press laws, and state sponsored persecution of local journalists.

Mr. M'Bai's online newspaper, the Freedom Newspaper had its main IP address blocked in the Gambia by the country's dictator Yahya Jammeh. People have been arrested, and tortured in the Gambia for merely surfing through his website. Although, there is no law put in place banning Gambians from accessing the Freedom Newspaper, but there were occasions, in which citizens caught reading the paper being detained and prosecuted on trumped up charges of communicating with a foreign journalist.

Beside English, Mr. M'Bai speaks three Gambian local languages: Wollof, Mandingka, and Fula. Mr. M'Bai lives in Raleigh, North Carolina.

Printed in Great Britain
by Amazon.co.uk, Ltd.,
Marston Gate.